CHURCH MUSIC

CHURCH MUSIC

A PRACTICAL HANDBOOK

BY

SYDNEY H. NICHOLSON

M.A., Mus. Bac.
Organist and Master of the Choristers
Westminster Abbey

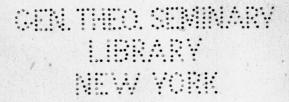
LONDON
THE FAITH PRESS
THE FAITH HOUSE, 22, BUCKINGHAM STREET, W.C. 2
MANCHESTER: 5 & 7, GREENGATE, SALFORD

CONTENTS

v

CHURCH MUSIC

CHAPTER I

MUSIC AND WORSHIP

FROM the earliest times Art, in some form or another, has been intimately associated with Public Worship. This association is perfectly natural, for on the one hand the very idea of Worship presupposes the giving of our best; and, on the other hand, the appeal of Art to the emotions is found to be one of the most powerful aids to devotion. So long as religion remains purely personal and subjective there is no need for outward expression: but such a frame of mind, with entire independence of externals, suffices for few; and to almost everyone some form of common worship becomes an essential part, as it is a clearly defined duty of their religion. The experience of past ages has taught most people the value, if not the actual need of some externals, or " aids to worship." There have been those who have tried to maintain that all such externals are merely distractions, and not aids at all; yet the Puritans could not do without their hymns, though they did throw down the organs and burn the surplices; and even those religious bodies which lay the greatest stress on the simplicity of their services have found that music is almost a necessity.

This intimate connection of music with worship is natural when it is remembered that music, in our modern sense of the word, actually grew up in the bosom of the Church, and that almost all the early developments of the Art from the crudest stages were due to its fostering care. Each of the great medieval Cathedrals and Abbeys had its own Song-School and its own staff of musicians; and in early times practically all serious musical enterprise was centred on these places. Indeed, it was not until a comparatively late period, somewhere about the middle of the sixteenth century, that there began to be any real distinction between secular and sacred music: in early times all the music there was, if we except folk-song, was Church music. When secular music branched off from the parent stock, the original tree did not, however, cease to grow and to bear fruit; and though the branch developed more quickly, so that it soon overshadowed the ancient stem, yet the vitality was still there, and leaves and blossoms were still forthcoming. No sooner had the divergence begun than it was found that progress in one uniform direction was no longer possible, and from that moment the element of style had its birth.

The new development on the secular side did not weaken the growth of Church music; a good deal of interest was, it is true, transferred from the sacred to the secular; but the two branches, though they diverged more and more widely, continued to interact the one on the other, to the great gain as well as to the partial loss of Church music. Early experiments, however, soon showed wise men that Church music, to serve its purpose, must have its own special style, and that the best style was the ancient. Palestrina wrote his immortal works in pursuance of these ideals, taking the old models and applying to them such of the new possibilities as were consistent with the pure style; and in his works, which may be regarded as representing the earliest school of organized Church music, we find more perfectly expressed than anywhere else a true standard of style. To Palestrina and his school all later Church music looks as its *fons et origo*. This is not to say that all good Church music is in the style of Palestrina; such a statement would be absurd; but it does mean that there has been no Church composer of note who has not felt the influence of this period, and in whose works it is not to some extent, however dimly, reflected.

So then we are brought to our first conclusion: *Church music must have a style of its own distinct from secular music*. The failure to observe this axiom has been responsible for many short-comings, and we need to-day, even more than in the sixteenth century, an edict to purge our Church music from secular influences. For such influences are rife, showing themselves equally in tawdry

Anthems and Services, which might as suitably
furnish settings for secular as sacred words; in
organ voluntaries selected from Wagner's operas,
or reminiscent of the music-hall march; in our
" revivalist " hymn tunes, with their suggestion
of " rag-time " or the dance.   One is familiar with
the plea that " the devil should not be allowed all
the best music "; one can only answer that it
would be a very good thing if a considerable
amount of our so-called sacred music were relegated
to his care!   Mere abuse, however, is of no avail,
and it will be more profitable to try and discover
what some of the elements of the true style of
Church music are.   A style cannot be defined in
a few words; were this possible there would be no
justification for the following pages, for the majority
of the subsequent chapters amount to little more
than an investigation of the different qualities
which, taken together, go to make up what we call
good style.

A second necessary characteristic of Church
music is that it must be the *outcome of a conscious
purpose*.   Ordinary music may, of course, be
written for some definite object, such as Opera of
dance music.   There is also a wide scope for
" absolute music "—that is to say, music which is
brought into existence merely as an expression of
beauty, apart altogether from its environment;
such music realizes its highest aims in forms like
the String Quartet, the Sonata or Symphony, and
is wholly independent of external circumstances.

But with Church music the case is otherwise; it must indeed, like all good art, conform to certain æsthetic laws, but in addition to this it demands the quality of fitness to its environment. Much music that would be wholly admirable in a concert-hall would be entirely out of place in a Church.

The conscious purpose underlying Church music may take various forms, some worthy and some unworthy.

Church music may be in itself intended as a pure act of worship; a definite offering to the Almighty of the best that can be given, alike by composer and performer. This is perhaps its highest aspect, and such a spirit should indeed underlie all music utilized in the service of God.

It may be regarded as an aid to devotion, in which direction all good art can serve a high and worthy end. Everyone who reads these words will be conscious of having at times felt a true thrill of inspiration at some splendid passage of music sung in the glorious surroundings of one of our great Cathedrals. Here the emotional appeal is very strongly pronounced, and few can be entirely unaffected by it: but the appeal may equally make itself felt in the humble surroundings of a village Church, at the most unexpected times. Who has not sometimes felt uplifted at the good congregational singing of a well-known hymn? The music may not be remarkable; the perform-ance, from the standard of the concert-room, may be execrable; but the appeal is there, and the conscious purpose of the music is making itself felt.

Church music may be intended as an attraction. This purpose, if rightly used, is not indefensible, provided that it is not the whole purpose. Were it wrong to use music as an attraction, how could we justify beauty in our buildings, or dignity in our ceremonial ? Beauty in all forms is a perfectly legitimate adjunct to religion, but to use beauty merely as a means of attraction and nothing else is quite wrong. An interesting programme is a complete justification for inducing people to go to a concert, but Church music has a higher purpose than that of bringing people into the House of God, nominally to take part in a religious Service, but really to attend a concert free of charge. The danger of introducing music merely as an attraction is a very real one, and is responsible for much in our Churches that had better not be there.

Church music may be intended for the gratification of the performers, and that of specially musical members of the congregation. Here again there is a danger. There is no harm, indeed there is much good, in a Choir singing or an Organist playing suitable music in Church, largely for their own pleasure and that of all who are specially interested. It is hard to find any reason why the idea of pleasure should be kept distinct from Church-going. Some people would seem to think that it is wrong to enjoy oneself in Church; but where can those who have been endowed with special gifts and special powers of appreciation better exercise them than in the House of Him who gave those gifts ? So that there would seem to be nothing radically wrong in using Church music as a means of pleasure. But the danger arises that some music, which is a pleasure to the performers and to some of the listeners, may equally be a distraction or a positive pain to others: so that this purpose of Church music needs to be guarded with a wise discretion.

Music is often introduced into Church Services merely as a concession to convention. In this case it is hardly introduced with any conscious purpose at all, except perhaps with that of imitating others and " doing the correct thing." There is hardly anything to be said for this practice, though it is terribly prevalent, and is responsible for the worst features of our Church music. It cannot too often be emphasized that *not a note of music is necessary to the performance of our Church Services ;* and it follows that every note that is introduced must have some definite and worthy purpose behind it. Far better no music at all than music which has no justification.

It appears, then, that in estimating the value of music in Church two tests should be applied:

Is the proposed music suitable for performance in Church ?

What is the reason for introducing it ?

On the answer to these two questions hangs the whole case for the use of music in our Services.

CHAPTER II

STYLE IN CHURCH MUSIC

In order that some idea may be formed as to what are the characteristics of the best styles of Church music, it is necessary to take a rapid survey of the historical aspect of the Art. It is outside the purpose of this book to deal with historical questions in detail, but some knowledge of the origins and development of Church music is necessary to anyone who wishes to obtain a real insight into the subject. For it is only by considering the best specimens of the Art at different stages that we can form any basis for criticism.

The history of Church music may be divided roughly into four periods:

1. The archaic period, dating from the earliest ages (for the origins of music are lost in antiquity), and extending roughly to the beginning of the sixteenth century, when music, as we now understand the term, began to emerge from the realms of tradition and folk-lore, and became an organized Art. In these early days there was little distinction between sacred and secular music, and though the English were held in high repute as a musical nation, and our early writers were reckoned as

14

pioneers, it cannot be said that there was any distinctive National School of Composition. Music was practically confined to unison melodies, or the crudest harmonic experiments, and such progress as was made was mainly due to the influence of the Church, which was practically the sole instrument of education and home of artistic culture. To this period belong the early plain-song settings of portions of the Liturgy, and the so-called Gregorian Tones. Harmony, as we know it, was practically non-existent, but towards the end of the period we see ever-increasing research, and a groping after some higher artistic development.

2. These strivings began to bear copious fruit early in the sixteenth century, at which date the second period may be said to commence. Music had become an organized Art; experiment had been succeeded by attainment; thought had become standardized, and a definite school of composition had been established. No sooner had this stage been reached than developments became rapid, and more advance was made in fifty years than had been achieved in the whole of past ages.

This late development of music as an organized Art, in comparison with the sister Arts of painting, sculpture, architecture or poetry, is a remarkable fact; and it is interesting to remember that at the time that music was first emerging from the embryo state, each one of the other Arts had reached, or even passed its zenith, and had developed a

technique to which subsequent ages have con-
tributed but little.

The early part of the period is characterized by
the attainment of a perfect grasp of pure choral
writing, and the central figure is Palestrina (1515-
1594). The school of which he is the greatest
representative relied for its effects on the simple
use of voices in harmony, with that independent
interest of the separate voice parts, technically
known as Counterpoint. A brief description of the
music of the period may be helpful. It was all
written for chorus, without solos or independent
instrumental accompaniment. It contains little of
what is commonly called "tune"; that is to say,
we never find a melody in the upper part with
mere accompanying chords below, but all the parts
are of approximately equal melodic interest. It
shows little tendency to reflect the sentiment of
the words except in a general sense; words are
constantly repeated, and the voices frequently sing
different words at the same time. It is in no
sense dramatic or illustrative; great use is made of
elaborate contrapuntal devices, such as " canons "
and " imitations "; and the music is highly scientific
though confined to a few simple chords. In fact,
much of it may be regarded as " absolute " music,
simply brought into existence as a thing of beauty,
the words being regarded mainly as a vehicle
for carrying beautiful sounds. Yet behind it all
lies an extraordinary religious feeling. No music
of any period is more perfectly adapted to the

human voice, or more completely fulfils the ideal
of what is appropriate for use in Church.   Calm,
austere, and wholly devoid of passion, it seems to
breathe the spirit of another world.

England produced many great masters who
worked on these lines, such as Christopher Tye
(c. 1508 - 1572), Richard Farrant (1530 - 1580),
Thomas Tallis (1520-1585), William Byrde (c. 1583-
1623), and Orlando Gibbons (1583-1625).

Early in this period had begun the independent
development of secular as distinct from sacred
music, and though the Church went on working on
the old lines, yet the new influence, particularly
the increasing interest shown in instrumental and
solo music, soon began to react on the older
methods; and towards the end of the period we
find that Church music has ceased to be purely
choral.   Instrumental accompaniments are tenta-
tively introduced; solo voices are employed; and
much that had been learnt from secular experiment
has been adopted by sacred Art.   So that by the
end of the sixteenth century an almost distinct
school of Church music had arisen; but this distinction was more marked in England than elsewhere, and for the following reason.   At the time
of the Reformation the English were keenly
interested in Church music, and had, as has already
been pointed out, produced several distinguished
composers.   So long as the Services had been
performed in Latin, the music of all countries
would be available; but with the establishment of

2

the English liturgy this was no longer the case, and music to suit the changed conditions had to be provided. The musicians at the time of change wrote both for the Latin and the English rite, while John Marbeck edited his famous " Praier Booke Noted "* (1550), mainly adapting the old Church melodies, that had been used with the Latin, to the English words.

Owing to this change of language and the consequent need for compositions by native musicians, a distinct school of English Church music may be said to have come into being at this time. The school had no sooner become organized and consolidated than another violent religious upheaval was experienced in the troublous times of the Stuarts. The period of the Commonwealth, with its Puritan tendencies, did much to check the flow of native Church music and for a time the chain was broken. Fortunately, however, the period was not long enough for the tradition to be lost, and at the time of the Restoration in 1660 there were a number of young musicians who were ready to link themselves to the past, and to continue to work also on fresh lines. Charles II. was interested in Church music, and during his residence abroad became imbued with a fondness for the lighter music of the French school where secular developments had been more rapid than in England; and through this influence a considerable change was effected in the style of our Church music. The use

* See below, p. 65.

of solo voices and independent accompaniments, extending even to long instrumental interludes, now becomes general, and at the same time the music loses much of its austerity. The greatest musicians of the time were Pelham Humfrey (1647-1674), (who on leaving the Chapel Royal Choir was sent by Charles II. to study under the French operatic composer Lully), Michael Wise (c. 1648-1687), John Blow (1648-1708), and above all, that greatest of English musicians, Henry Purcell (1658-1695). The music of these men is far more dramatic and illustrative than that of the earlier writers; there is far more attempt to suit the music to the words; the whole method is far more free; but, except in a few specimens, there is nothing like the same purity in the choral writing. However, their music is instinct with true Church style, and the spirit of the earlier writers is felt to be still alive and bearing good fruit.

By the end of the period our Liturgy had become more or less fixed, and the places at which music was required had become recognized. These consisted mainly of "Services," or settings of the Canticles at Morning and Evening Prayer with certain portions of the Communion Office, and the Anthem. But at this time a minor, though important branch of the Art began to make its appearance in the "Psalm-tunes" which were provided for the metrical versions of the Psalms then in use. Much splendid work was done in this direction, and many of the finest hymn-tunes we use to-day date from this period. The Prayer-Book version of the Psalms was probably chanted in but few places, and exactly how they were treated is somewhat obscure. It is, however, clear that where they were sung, some of the old Gregorian Tones were used at first, though experiments were being made in the direction of recurring harmonized settings, which gradually developed into the regular Anglican Chant.

3. By the end of the seventeenth century the art of music had reached a stage of comparative maturity. All the forms which we now know, including opera, oratorio, song, chamber, and orchestral music, had been developed to various degrees; and in the matter with which we are chiefly concerned, the school of English Church music had become firmly established, and had produced some of its most remarkable composers.

In the year 1685 two giant composers, Handel and Bach, were born—the two composers who, more than any others, were destined to influence the future course of Church music. The stupendous work of Bach was, during his lifetime, known only to few, and those his own countrymen; and it was not until he was rediscovered at a later period that his influence became so wide. But Handel was by no means content that his light should remain hidden under a bushel. After various wanderings he settled down in England in 1710, and later became a naturalized British subject; and it was in this country that he produced his most important works and achieved his greatest fame. Unfortunately the time of his arrival happened to coincide with a period when there was no English composer of outstanding genius. Purcell had just died in 1695 (when, be it noted, Handel and Bach were only ten years old), and there was no one to take his place. The reigning House of Hanover, moreover, was favourable to things foreign. From these and other causes it came about that contemporary English music was practically swallowed up in the overwhelming embrace of Handel, and his influence was so strong that it took our native art a century to shake itself free from it.

No one can question the wonderful genius of Handel at his best, but no composer more than he suffered from success, and much of the work he turned out was quite ordinary, and unworthy of the composer of " The Messiah." His imitators as usual caught his mannerisms without his genius, so that much feeble and unoriginal stuff was produced, and in no department of Art was this more pronounced than in the music of the Church. All honour then to such men as Croft, Greene, Boyce, Battishill, and a few others, who, though they were considerably influenced by Handel, yet did keep the national style alive, and wrote a certain amount of music well worthy to hold its place with the best works of the past.

At this period began the growth of the hymn-tune proper, as distinct from the severe psalm-tune of the earlier age. The introduction of the metrical hymn into our service, as distinct from the paraphrased psalm, was due largely to Nonconformist influences, and demanded the composition of many new tunes; so that the eighteenth century produced a highly characteristic school of hymn-tunes. The worst of these were very poor specimens, relying on florid embellishments of the most feeble kind for whatever effect they produced; but the period also gave birth to a far superior style of hymn-tune, marked by much elegance and grace, and in some cases by great melodic beauty, so that it is to this period we may also look for some of the best of our tunes. The eighteenth century also saw the development of the Anglican chant into an organized and definite musical form, showing much the same characteristics as the hymn-tune.

Perhaps the hymn-tune and the Anglican chant are the most notable contributions of the eighteenth century to our Church music. The stirring events that were happening in the world of music in other countries had, during the domination of Handel, little effect here. The work of great masters like Haydn, Mozart, or Gluck for the moment counted for little; in fact we were at this time exceedingly insular, and had it not been for the faithful handful of Church musicians, native art would almost have died out.

4. The nineteenth century soon gave promise of better things. Freed at last from the long thral-

dom of Handelian tradition, Church musicians were ready to examine and learn from what had been done elsewhere. The pioneer of the new style, or perhaps rather the connecting link between the eighteenth century and the new school, was Thomas Attwood (1765-1838). He had been a pupil of Mozart, whose influence was often to be traced in his work, and he wrote a good deal of secular as well as sacred music. He was not a great composer, but the interesting point about his Church compositions is that he evidently did try to infuse new vitality and more modern methods into his work. He was, however, quickly succeeded by far abler men, such as Samuel Wesley (1766-1837), William Crotch (1775-1847), Thomas Attwood Walmisley (1814-1856), and Samuel Sebastian Wesley (1810-1876), all of whom, and especially the latter, brought modern influences to bear on the old methods, and while still conserving the old national style, infused it with new life and inspiration. Now at last we begin to find traces of the influence of Bach, the greatest of all Church musicians, and this influence, which was largely fostered by the efforts of Mendelssohn and his friends, was destined to have a powerful effect on all subsequent Church music. From this point to an ever-increasing degree our Church music ceases to be isolated from the main currents of the musical thought of the day; stagnation, which is the inevitable result of isolation, ceases, and instead we get consistent progress.

There seems, however, to be a fatality hanging over the music of this country, in its preference for things foreign, whether composers or performers, and we have never seemed capable of taking our own native art quite seriously. Whatever may be the cause it is a fact that English music has again and again been almost captured by foreigners. The most notable example, of course, is the Handel régime, but for its effect on Church music, the Mendelssohn worship, which now came into fashion, was almost as potent. National art was just ready to assert itself after its long period of quiescence, but hardly yet strong enough to develop on distinct lines of its own, so it was quite natural that a new style, and one so attractive as that of Mendelssohn, should find many admirers and imitators. As much of his best work was sacred music, it was to be expected that his influence would be most marked in this direction: so that at this time we find a strong access of the romantic to our previously unemotional and somewhat formal idiom. At its best this new influence finds expression in the immortal works of S. S. Wesley; at its worst it has no small responsibility for those hosts of feeble platitudes whose only merit is a certain superficial prettiness. But in spite of all that may be said against it, the Mendelssohn influence did great service to our Church music by bringing to it an ideal of real life and sincerity, as well as in helping to transmit the Bach tradition.

The influence of other great composers of the day, such as Beethoven, Schubert, Schumann, Wagner, and Brahms, though less direct, has made itself felt in all branches of the Art, and to this Church music is no exception. But there are two minor composers whose influence was quite out of proportion to their importance; these are Spohr and Gounod. Both of these composers could write good music, but each of them evolved certain mannerisms, pleasant enough in their way, especially when they were new, yet soon worn threadbare: woefully weak when badly imitated, yet fatally easy of imitation. And the sickly chromaticism and weak sentimentality to be found in so many of the compositions of the Victorian Church musicians is largely to be attributed to the influence of these composers. The group of which Stainer and Barnby are the best representatives derived more from these mediocre writers than from their great predecessors in the English school. At the same time there is too great a tendency to disparage their work to-day, much of which is quite sound if rather uninspired, while Stainer especially could at times write really fine and noble music, as, for instance, his anthem " I saw the Lord." They and their school were to some extent the victims of circumstance; the " Catholic revival," productive as it was of so much that was good, brought in its train certain developments which were not unmixed blessings. The general introduction of Choirs and Choral Services in almost every town and village created a sudden demand for music which was effective and at the same time easy; and this naturally called for the efforts of those musicians prominently associated with the movement. The demand soon produced a copious supply, and if much of it is now better consigned to oblivion, still some of it may remain as an earnest endeavour to meet the circumstances of its day. The national line of development was more consistently carried on by such men as Sir John Goss, Sir Frederick Gore Ouseley, George Garrett, and Edward Hopkins.

Of contemporary writers it is obviously impossible to speak, but it may safely be said that a stage has been reached when our Church music is never likely to be dominated by the idiosyncrasies of any one composer, though it has come into line with other branches of the Art sufficiently to be affected by every current of contemporary thought. Everything then promises well for its continuance and progress on truly national lines.

CHAPTER III

TYPES OF MUSICAL SERVICE

In endeavouring to decide what form of Church music is best adapted for our Services to-day, it is necessary that a clear distinction should be drawn between those Churches where the music should be confined to the simplest, and those where more elaboration is justified. To ape a Cathedral Service in a village Church is the height of absurdity, yet there are Parish Churches in large places which are themselves Cathedral-like in structure, and where an efficient Choir and Organ are attainable; and in these the Services may be fashioned far more nearly on Cathedral lines. Probably, however, the largest number of Churches will occupy an intermediate position between these two extremes, demanding something more than the barest simplicity, yet for a variety of causes finding the full choral Service beyond their attainments and beyond their desire. It should be possible, then, to distinguish three main types of musical Service, suitable not only for Churches of different character, but for different Services in the same Church.

First of all, however, it is necessary to consider

briefly the resources available, for on this depends much. Practically every Church in the land possesses some kind of musical instrument for accompaniment purposes; indeed this is a practical necessity, for unaccompanied singing presents a good deal of difficulty to any but a well-trained choir. The instrument in a small Church is generally either a harmonium, an American organ, or a small pipe organ, perhaps with one manual and pedals: when this provision is all that is possible, only the simplest music should be attempted. Any Church aspiring to a regular " musical service " should have an organ with at least two manuals and pedals, and in a larger Church we shall expect to find three or four manuals. Let it here be said that even the smallest pipe organ is infinitely better than any other instrument for Church purposes: failing this a harmonium is better than an American organ, the feeble, snuffling tone of which is extremely tiresome, and does not serve well to support voices. A pianoforte would be far better than either of these two instruments, both in musical effect and for the purpose of leading the singing; but for some reason the piano is considered to be a profane instrument, though it is hard to imagine what can be the sacred associations of its more favoured rivals.

Then as to Choir. Theoretically it should be possible to do without a Choir at all, if the music is confined to the simplest things; but practically it is found that the singing is apt to be fainthearted and apathetic unless there are some definite leaders. The composition of the Choir is, for the present, immaterial; but it would seem to be a practical necessity that in any Church where music is to be employed as a regular part of the Services, there should be a Choir of some sort: what sort it should be will be considered later.

Thirdly, there must be some person or persons responsible for playing the organ and instructing the Choir; the two offices may be combined in one, as they often are. The first qualification for the organist obviously is that he or she should be able to play the instrument correctly, and for the Choirmaster that he or she should have sufficient knowledge of music to be able to instruct others. But these qualifications are not always to be found in a village community, and when this is so, and no one can be found to play who is able to do so correctly, then it is quite clear that no music should be attempted, for it should be an axiom that no music at all is infinitely better than bad music. A literal observance of this principle might mean the silencing of the music in some few village Churches, but not in very many, for nearly always someone can be found who can play correctly up to the difficulty of an ordinary hymn-tune. And if this standard of attainment can be reached it is quite sufficient, provided that nothing more is attempted. The guiding principle in all cases should be *never to ask from an Organist or a Choir more than they can do properly*.

Before trying to decide what sort of Church music is suitable for different kinds of Churches, or at particular Services, it will be well once more to affirm the cardinal principle that *no music is necessary* in Church, from which it follows that every note that is introduced must be justified by some conscious purpose.

Bearing this in mind, the conditions may first be considered which might reasonably obtain in any small village Church, where it is desirable to introduce music. The first thing to start with is undoubtedly hymns. Hymn-singing is certainly the most popular as well as the easiest part of Choral Worship, and a Service may be infinitely brightened and beautified by the introduction of hymns alone. This can be managed successfully even in the humblest Church; anything beyond this demands a greater measure of skill on the part of the player and singers. The music, then, in the simplest Services should consist solely of hymn-singing in unison, and, be it added, in a key which is not too high for untrained voices. In certain hymn-books some of the tunes are set too high for this purpose, but the difficulty may be got over by providing the Organist with a transposed copy; such an edition is issued for *Hymns Ancient and Modern*, and this alone contains some six hundred tunes in suitable keys.

The next addition to the music should be chants for the Canticles. If chanting is restricted to these, it will present little difficulty, owing to the frequency of their repetition. Whether Anglican or Gregorian chants are used is for the present immaterial, but the chants selected should be in suitable keys, of moderate compass, without high reciting notes, and of real melodic interest so as to be suitable for unison singing. For in the simplest Services part-singing should not even be dreamt of.

The next musical addition should be the singing of the responses: but the artistic possibility of this depends upon certain conditions. The first is the necessity of the Priest's part being properly sung. The effect of the versicle being said or monotoned, and the response sung, cannot be considered satisfactory; at the same time it is better than when the Priest's part is sung badly. If the Priest is musical and can take his part correctly, no difficulty arises; but if he is not musical, a sung response necessitates an instrumental accompaniment. It is quite against tradition that responses should be accompanied, and the effect of the constant entry of the organ for a few chords is most unpleasing. And if accompanied responses are objectionable, what is to be said of accompanied Amens ? what can be more ridiculous than that every prayer throughout the Service should conclude with two common chords on the organ ? If, then, the Priest is unable to sing his part, the versicles and responses are best said, and the same of course applies to the Litany and the Amens. But there is one possible solution of the difficulty—

namely, that it should be competent for a Choirman to sing the versicles. This is the regular
practice in some Cathedrals in the case of the
Litany: a Lay-reader, when duly authorized, is
permitted to take all those parts of the Service
where singing is involved: it is hard, therefore, to
see why this permission should not be extended
to any suitable Choirman under special circumstances. Indeed, such a course has been adopted
in some cases " with the approval of the Ordinary,"
and would seem analogous to the practice of
allowing a layman to read the Lessons.

The position may be summarized as follows:
The responses clearly ought, if possible, to be
sung, and they certainly ought not to be accompanied. This necessitates the versicles being sung
as well as the responses; and if the Priest cannot
sing, someone ought to be allowed to do so in his
stead. This would at once solve the difficulty in
most cases.

If the responses are to be sung, and it is regarded
as a *sine quâ non* that they should be sung unaccompanied, there are two possible courses: they
may be sung in unison or in harmony. In ninety-
nine cases out of a hundred harmony is attempted,
even with an incomplete Choir; and to get something like a decent effect this is bolstered up with
an accompaniment. Few seem to realize how
much better it is, except with a highly trained
Choir, that the responses should be sung in simple
unison without accompaniment. No one wishes

or expects the Priest's inflections to be accompanied, yet precisely the same inflections when sung by the Choir are always required to be harmonized. It is hard to see the reason for this, for if the effect of a single voice without accompaniment is not too thin and bare, surely it is less so with a number of voices. If the practice of singing the plain-song of the responses in unison, without accompaniment, and regarding them merely as free inflections of the voice and not as little tunes in strict time, were given a fair trial, it is probable that it would soon become the established use, and people would not wish to return to the harmonized form.

This spontaneous and devotional rendering of the responses may well be adopted by any Choir, with the proviso that the versicles can be sung by the Priest, or by a duly authorized layman; but this does not carry with it any justification for the dangerous practice of the perpetual use of the monotone. This custom has little to commend it, and it has been greatly abused. In the majority of Churches the monotone is employed from beginning to end of the Service. Two arguments are commonly used in support of it: First, that it prevents that kind of familiar or semi-dramatic recitation of the prayers which used to be rather common. Second, that it enables the voice to carry better in a large building. To the first point the obvious answer is that it is certain that those who favour the particular kind of reading

3

referred to would never be induced to adopt the monotone under any circumstances; to the second, that if it is necessary to employ the monotone to make the words of the prayers audible—words which are already perfectly familiar to everyone present—why is it not necessary to employ it for the Lessons and the Sermon, the words of which are comparatively unfamiliar ? The sooner promiscuous monotoning is given up, the better, musically, and in every other way. Indulgence in this practice is largely responsible for that " Church drawl," so detested of the laity, and its abandonment, where it is not necessary, would tend to increased congregations and a more reverent and genuine rendering of the Services. There may be something to be said for it in a great Cathedral, where the Choral Service from beginning to end should move along as a continuous whole: again, a frequent change from the singing to the speaking voice is apt to be disturbing, so that where the responses are sung it is best to keep to the monotone for the prayers which are contiguous to them. A suitable use prevails in some Dioceses, which might well become general. Everything is read till the versicle " O Lord, open Thou our lips "; then singing or monotoning prevails till the third collect, followed by the Anthem or Hymn; and after this the natural voice is resumed (the Amens being simply said).

The same principle applies, of course, to the

prayers in which the congregation join audibly with the Priest. It is far better, usually, that these should be said in a natural voice rather than monotoned. Not only is the practice itself desirable, as tending to greater reality, but it avoids one great difficulty: the maintenance of pitch on the monotone is a task which taxes the capabilities of even the best Cathedral Choirs, and it is one that is hardly ever consistently achieved in an ordinary Church. Any but the best monotoning is painful to a person with a musical ear, and it is surely unwise, from a desire to follow a needless convention, that Choirs should be confronted with a difficulty that it is most unlikely that they will be able to master. At least, if monotoning is demanded, let it be on a low note: the favourite G is too high to be comfortable for average voices, and the effect is less objectionable if a lower note is chosen.

The next addition to the music would naturally be the singing of the Psalms. This presents far greater difficulties, whatever the system employed, than anything hitherto dealt with. The ideal musical treatment of the Psalter has yet to be discovered, and every system, be it Anglican or plain-song, is very greatly dependent upon the intelligence of the performers. It may almost be said that a good Choir will chant well with any system of pointing, and a bad Choir will be successful with none. The question of Anglican and Gregorian chants will be considered later: suffice it to say here that the chanting of the Psalms should only be introduced with great caution, and where a Choir is really good; also that harmonized singing is by no means necessary, and unison is often much better. But it must be remembered that no singing of the Psalms is really congregational, and congregations are hardly ever to be found which really manage the pointing properly: in the first place they are not generally supplied with pointed Psalters, and even if they had them they would be useless without considerable practice. This means that the bulk of the singing is thrown on the Choir. Now good chanting is the greatest difficulty that has to be faced even by a Cathedral Choir which sings the Psalms every day; how much more difficult, then, for an ordinary Parish Choir which only sings them once a week: and how absolutely impossible for a congregation that never practises them at all. Still, the Psalms undoubtedly ought to be sung, if possible, and the trouble spent on their careful preparation will be amply repaid by the beautiful results that can be obtained by patient study and practice.

When we have got to the chanting of the Psalms, the next step would naturally be some slightly different settings for the Canticles. It is evident that these portions should receive rather more decorative treatment than the ordinary daily Psalms; but in most Churches the elaborate " Service " setting is to be deprecated. Yet something is needed beyond the normal chant: for one thing, the " Te Deum " especially does not lend itself to ordinary pointing, and the " Nunc dimittis " is suited little better. A solution may perhaps be looked for in the direction of " Chant Services," or the simple old-fashioned Services of the Cathedral type, without repetition of words, and without solos and elaboration of any sort. Services of this kind, if constantly repeated, may be learnt by congregations as well as by Choirs in quite a short time, almost as readily as hymn-tunes. A good plan in an ordinary Church is to have in use a cycle of four or five such Service settings, and to use them over and over again till they become quite familiar.

This, however, presupposes a Choir which can sing in harmony, that is where all the parts are represented with a reasonable degree of efficiency: for these Services are set compositions dependent for their effect on harmony, and it is inartistic to sing them in unison. Unison Services do, of course, exist, and may be used by unison Choirs; but where ordinary Services of the type mentioned are employed, they require harmony, and should not be used where the Choir is not complete.

The same principles apply to settings of the Communion Office. Unison Services should be the invariable rule unless complete harmony can be supplied. Chant Services for the Communion Office are unfortunately almost out of the question, and very few have been written successfully: but Communion Services can be quite simple, and though there are not many of these, there are enough, and the need for more could easily be supplied if the demand arose. But so long as the preference for cheap effect remains prevalent, so long will the kind of thing be turned out which brings reproach upon our Church music, but royalties into the pockets of unscrupulous composers and avaricious publishers. A well-rendered Choral Communion can be the highest expression of worship in music that is attainable: but bad or indifferent rendering here, more than at any other time, strikes a jarring note. The beautiful rendering of a Choral Eucharist should be the highest aim of a Choir, but the privilege of attempting it should not be granted them until they have thoroughly proved their capacity in other directions. Here is no place for experiments, or even for well-intentioned attempts: excellence is demanded, and anything short of it is failure.

Having gone so far it will be allowable to introduce an occasional Anthem: and if the Choir has mastered all the difficulties enumerated, this further addition will present little difficulty. But the choice of Anthems should be exercised with the greatest care, for the number of bad ones on the market is extraordinary. Excellent Anthems, for all seasons and of all degrees of difficulty, are available, if only people will find them out. Here again reticence is necessary, and the temptation offered by the " easy and effective " style of composition must be resisted. The Anthem is a luxury and entirely unnecessary: so there is not the smallest justification for it on any grounds at all unless it is edifying. The wisdom of the frequent introduction of Anthems in Parish Churches is questionable. Unless they are really good compositions and well sung, they are apt to cause a good deal of distress to the congregation: yet they are an interest to the Choir, who, after all, deserve some consideration. Probably it would often be better that the Choir, instead of producing frequent Anthems, should spread the study over a longer time, and tackle some larger work such as a Cantata or portion of an Oratorio, and then perform it at a special musical Service.

There is one other feature of the musical Service which must receive some slight consideration, as it is of almost universal use. This is the organ Voluntary. Provided that a Voluntary is well chosen and well played on a good instrument, it may be a most helpful ornament to the Service—but only if the above conditions are fulfilled: and in very many cases, where the instrument is poor, or the player unskilful, it would be much better that it should be dispensed with altogether. Incoherent progressions on a wheezy harmonium are not calculated to attune the heart to a spirit of worship; and the vulgar commonplaces of a " festal march " strike a jarring note after the final words of Benediction, which does much to destroy the solemnity of the whole Service. It is not possible to deal with this matter here with the fulness that it deserves.* It must suffice to say that the same test should be applied to the Voluntary as to all the other parts of the Church music: Does it add to the beauty of the Service, or does it not ? It need hardly be said that a Voluntary is in no way necessary. Even with a surpliced Choir a " processional entry " is not requisite, and it is quite seemly for them to enter their places quietly just before the commencement of Service. Even though it may not be liturgically correct, an opening hymn sung as the Choir come into Church is infinitely better than a bad Voluntary: but there is much to be said for reserving the first sound of music till the words " O Lord, open Thou our lips," or " O come, let us sing unto the Lord."

Each element has now been briefly dealt with that goes to make up the " full Cathedral Service." It is impossible to say exactly how much or how little should be sung in any particular Church, as so much depends upon the particular conditions, and the material available; but a safe guiding principle in all cases is, Sing less than you might, and do not sing anything at all unless it is certain that it would be better sung than said.

It should, however, be possible to distinguish a

* For a fuller discussion of this subject, see the author's pamphlet, " The Organ Voluntary," Church Music Society's " Occasional Papers," No. 6. Humphrey Milford. 2d.

little more clearly the three types of Service to which reference was made at the beginning of the Chapter, and to summarize the main requirements and limitations of each:

1. Simplest form of Musical Service.

Material.—A small Choir to lead the singing; a small organ, pianoforte, or harmonium; an Organist who can play music of the difficulty of a hymn-tune correctly.

Possibilities.—Hymns; chanted Canticles; Responses (if the Versicles can be sung); in more advanced cases Psalms and occasional unison Services. All the singing to be in unison, unless complete harmony can be maintained.

2. The normal Parish Church Service.

Material.—A Choir in which all the four parts are represented, and which is reasonably well balanced; an organ with at least two manuals and pedals; an Organist who can play all the music required correctly, and a Choirmaster who has a good ear and a sufficient knowledge of the technique of choral singing.

Possibilities.—Hymns; Responses (unaccompanied, either harmony or unison); Psalms; Canticles (Chant Services or simple settings often repeated); simple Communion Services; occasional Anthems; occasional Cantatas or Oratorios.

3. The full Cathedral Service.

Material.—A Church of suitable type; a really good Choir, represented in each part by trained singers; a good organ of sufficient size; a thoroughly competent professional Organist and Choirmaster.

Possibilities.—The whole range of Church music.

CHAPTER IV

QUIRES AND PLACES WHERE THEY SING

THERE are those who say that Choirs are a nuisance, and that Church music would be better without them. But as a matter of fact it is found that they are not only a practical necessity, but that if rightly dealt with they are an enormous gain and a powerful agency for good. Few congregations will be found which will, except on special occasions, maintain the singing heartily, firmly, and in a musical manner, without the leadership of a Choir. The singing of any but large congregations, with very well-known music, will soon become listless and disorderly.

Taking it for granted, then, that a Choir of some sort is a practical necessity, it will be useful to consider the constitution of the Choir under different circumstances. Taking once more the three types of Service already distinguished, it will be found that a different kind of Choir is suitable for each.

But first of all a word or two as to the constitution of Choirs in general.

For the formation of a Choir the available material consists of men, boys, women or girls.

43

It is obvious that the employment of men is necessary in a Choir that aims at completeness, but for the upper parts there are alternatives.

In favour of the employment of women the chief argument is that their voices are settled and not subject to " breaking." The fact that they have arrived at years of discretion may be expected to solve some difficulties in the matter of behaviour, and they should come to their work with a more mature sense of responsibility.

In favour of the employment of young girls is the fact that their voices do not suddenly become useless at the period of adolescence, but the difficulties in the way of training and discipline are equal to those experienced with boys.

In favour of the employment of boys so many arguments can be adduced, that they would seem to outweigh all the supposed disadvantages. When boys cannot be obtained women or girls may well be employed, but the following points should be remembered:

(*a*) The employment of boys is not only traditionally correct from an ecclesiastical standpoint, but the work itself may be a valuable force in the formation of a boy's character, and further it is practically the only piece of definite Church work that a boy can do.

(*b*) The voices of women, unless they are exceptionally well trained, do not usually blend well in small numbers: the greater strength of the individual voices causes any faults of particular singers to be painfully apparent and easily to destroy the beauty of the general effect.

(c) The voices of boys are as a rule far preferable in quality to those of girls of a similar age.

(d) A mixture of girls' and boys' voices does not usually form a good blend.

(e) The quality of well-trained boys' voices, with its freedom from artificial sentiment and its impersonal as distinct from individualistic effect, is exactly what is most suitable for Church music; and it was in view of a rendering by boys' voices that all our best Church music was written.

(f) The only serious drawback is the breaking of the voice at a period when a boy has just reached his maximum usefulness, with the consequent need of keeping a continuous supply of boys in training. As to matters of discipline and reverence, these are certainly not more difficult to overcome with a properly handled choir of boys than they are in a choir of any other constitution.

So that there is almost everything to be said for the employment of boys for the treble part in a choir; but with the alto part it is different. Boy altos are seldom satisfactory, and the low " chest notes " of boys do not, unless specially well trained, blend well in the harmony. Men altos are by far the most satisfactory for Church music, and all the standard compositions were written with this voice in view. But good men altos are rare, and it may often be the wisest course to employ women for the alto part.

It should be possible in almost any village to find sufficient boys to form all the choir that is necessary or desirable; in a small Church ten or twelve will be enough. It should in such cases be laid down clearly that all singing is to be in unison, and then the Choirboys become simply the leaders of the congregation: if they sing clearly, rhythmically, and well in tune, no men will be needed to help them. The congregation are not expected to sing in harmony, and a far better lead will be given if the organized singers simply concentrate on the melody. In this way all the music referred to as suitable for the simplest type of Service can be rendered adequately and artistically. In any village Church or small parish, Choirmen should only be introduced after very mature reflection. It is not that Choirmen are undesirable, indeed they are absolutely essential to a complete choir, and as a whole they are a most enthusiastic and self-sacrificing body of Church workers. But the dangers of introducing them in a small parish are so great that they must be carefully weighed. The first danger is that the number of men available will necessarily be few: if they are lost they probably cannot be replaced; therefore their wishes will of necessity exercise an undue influence on those in authority. Choirmen do not as a rule like singing in unison, nor do they desire to confine their efforts to the simplest things: their natural enthusiasm and ambition often lead them to wish to attempt music which is beyond the powers, if not of themselves, at any rate of the choir as a whole. If once harmony is introduced a proper balance of parts is an absolute necessity, and the material to insure this is hardly likely to be forthcoming in a small community. Without in any way wishing to disparage the work of Choirmen as a class, it may safely be said that nine-tenths of the difficulties connected with small choirs are due to the senior members. So that under conditions where only the simplest music is required, it is strongly recommended that choirs should consist of boys only: and even where something more ornate is desired, there are possibilities in the direction of part-singing for treble voices, which may serve the purpose better than a four-part effort by an ill-balanced choir containing men.

Turning to the second type, which may be regarded as the normal Parish Church Service, we are dealing with another set of conditions. Here it may reasonably be expected that a sufficiency of material will be available for the formation and maintenance of a complete choir. But the difficulties are increased rather than lessened, and it is absolutely necessary that such a choir should be subject to a certain amount of discipline. That this is the case with regard to the boys is self-evident, but it is often not recognized that it is even more necessary with the men.

Most of the choirs in question will be voluntary, that is to say unpaid as far as the men are concerned; but nevertheless one strict rule will be necessary if there is to be any prospect of success. This is that each member of the choir must understand that his regular attendance at all Services and practices is an essential condition of his membership: and should he be irregular in attendance, the authorities must face the unpleasant task that will fall upon them of asking him to vacate his position. Further, they must be prepared to do this in *every* case, however valuable the individual voice, or whatever the social position or moral worth of the person may be. If this task cannot be faced—and it is one that is sure sooner or later to cause some unpleasantness—it is better to do without any men at all. But if the rule once becomes a recognized obligation of choir work, as it is in the best choral societies, it will *ipso facto* cease to need application. Many choirs are ruined by failure to carry out this principle: a Vicar will hesitate to dismiss a Choirman " because he is a Sidesman," or " because his daughters are Sunday-school teachers," or for fifty other reasons; whereas the only consideration should be whether his remaining a member of the choir tends to increase its efficiency or otherwise. One Choirman who is irregular in his attendance may ruin the efforts of a good choir and unfortunately some of the worst offenders are frequently found amongst the men who have the best voices.

The Organist and Choirmaster now becomes a

factor of great importance. Not *any one* will do:
it is necessary that the office should be held by
someone who, in musical ability, is superior to
those whom he will have to instruct; otherwise
there is little chance of his being able to win their
respect. And, further, the Choirmaster must be
possessed of a gift for teaching: he must be able
to work his choir hard without boring them; he
must be thorough without wasting time; he must
be a firm disciplinarian without alienating his
voluntary workers; he must possess the power of
criticism not only of others but of himself. Among
those who take up the work it is possible to find
quite a large number who can play the organ well,
compared to those who can train a choir; yet
there is no question as to which part of the work
is the more important. No degree of excellence
in the playing of fugues will make up for defective
methods in choir-training. The capacity is to
some extent innate, but much more careful preparation should be given to the study of this side
of the work than is usual. In most cases the
young Organist has to buy his own experience, and
has very little opportunity of guidance from those
who have been through the mill.

Assuming that a Church has a good and well-
balanced choir, regular in attendance, and with
a good reserve of material, a competent Organist
and a good organ, it might seem that the musical
prospects were serene. And so they may well be:
but nevertheless there will probably be some

breakers ahead. Most likely the first of these will be the desire of the choir to introduce more and more ornate music. This is the peculiar snare of the voluntary choir, and of the gifted, though possibly inexperienced organist. The reason is not far to seek: such people are easily satisfied with a standard of performance, which judged by the highest standards, is only mediocre. They are unable to see how much better it might be, and not knowing how to go any further with one particular piece of work they naturally wish, for the sake of variety, to turn to something fresh. Consequently there is a tendency to increase the repertoire rather than to polish up the rendering. With the best choirs and organists this is not the case: their aim lies not so much in the direction of performing a great deal of music, as of concentrating their attention on doing a little very well. This very common desire to introduce fresh music is a considerable source of annoyance to many members of congregations, and rightly so. A choir can find all its legitimate aspirations realized in the effort to give a perfect rendering of simple things; and the truest criterion of a good choir is not how it sings an Anthem, but how it sings the Psalms, and the plain parts of the Service which are repeated every Sunday.

Another difficulty experienced with choirs is that they are apt to have " feelings." It is right that encouragement should be given to choirs, but they are too apt to think themselves indispensable, and to resent anything in the nature of criticism, even though it is perfectly deserved and tactfully administered.

Then again a regular choir, whether voluntary or paid, necessitates a certain amount of expense. Books and music and their necessary renewal alone cost a certain amount of money. Also it is usually found best to give the Choirboys something tangible in the way of rewards or small payments, and even adult members are not above the joys of choir picnics. The Organist, too, should receive a salary that is in some measure adequate to the work he is expected to do. Organists' salaries are miserable at the best, but it is absolutely wrong to expect a man to produce a good musical Service at a stipend of £20 or £30 a year.

All these things ought to be faced, for it is useless to have a choir unless there is means for keeping it going properly: a bad equipment is fatal to success: fragmentary music books, dirty surplices or torn cassocks, do not tend to efficiency.

But on the other side of the picture there is a very encouraging outlook. The choir can form, under proper conditions, one of the brightest spots of Church life in a parish. In no other way is it possible to exercise a greater influence for good on the members than through the agency of a well-ordered choir. Nothing contributes so greatly to the beauty, the reverence, and the attractiveness of a Service as good music. So that the trouble that has to be faced is amply worth while; only it is useless to pretend that it can be avoided altogether, or that what is so desirable can be obtained without any difficulty.

The Full Choral Service demands not only a thoroughly competent and experienced organist, but a highly trained choir. It should only be attempted in Cathedrals or College Chapels, or in a few Parish Churches of a Cathedral-like type. It almost necessarily involves considerable expense, for it is practically necessary that not only the boys but the men should be paid: the demands on their time will otherwise be too great to be reasonable. There is no limit to the amount or elaboration of the music that can be rendered under these conditions: it need only be pointed out once more that the best Choirs aim far less at elaboration than perfection of detail. Such a Choir, in its proper surroundings, is the crowning beauty of the Church Service. It is not suitable in all places, but in its true home, the Cathedral, it is incomparable; it is the perfect complement of splendid architecture, dignified ceremonial and eloquent preaching; and just as these, it brings its own peculiar message which may stir the heart of many a worshipper in a way that nothing else can.

Before leaving the subject of Choirs, a few thoughts on choir management may be helpful.

Perhaps the most important matter in the musical activities of a Church is the method in which the Choir-practices are conducted. Circumstances vary, and sometimes it is necessary that all rehearsals should be in Church; in other places a Vestry or other adjacent room is available. Whenever possible some room should be provided in which most of the rehearsals, at any rate those for the boys, can be held. The ideal arrangement is a fairly large room which serves the purpose of a Practice Room, a Choirboys' Vestry, and a Music Library. Such a room should, if possible, be provided with desks similarly arranged to those in Church: it is then possible for each boy to have his own " place," and rehearsals and robing can be carried out in an orderly fashion, while no delay is experienced in fetching and carrying music. If a proper Practice Room cannot be provided, much work must needs be done in Church which is better done elsewhere.

The proper instrument for use at Choir-practice is undoubtedly a Piano: a Harmonium or American Organ is about the worst substitute, as it induces a bad tone, and by its sustaining quality covers up defects and makes them harder to recognize. Failing a Piano, the next best thing is some small portable instrument, such as the "Dulcitone," which produces its sounds by striking on tuning forks, and has the great advantage of possessing a beautifully clear though soft tone, and also of not getting out of tune.

Choirs, and particularly Choirboys, need a good deal of instruction in such matters as sight-reading and voice-production, involving scales and exercises and so forth. Though these are a necessary means to an end, it is difficult to connect them in a boy's mind directly with the idea of definite religious work: it is far better to approach them from a purely secular standpoint, and to reserve for the Church only such rehearsal as has a direct bearing on the Service. Further, it is a great advantage if the boys' practices can be enlivened by the use of a good deal of secular music. Secular songs are just as valuable as sacred music for purposes of training, and afford a welcome relief both to boys and master, while the repetition of sacred words merely as technical studies is avoided. Furthermore, in a secular building use may be made of any sense of humour which the Choir-master is happy enough to possess, a faculty which will contribute greatly to his success in handling boys, but which in Church is obviously entirely out of place.

There should be an absolute distinction of method between practices in Church and those in the practice room. All practices in Church should be conducted with the same decorum as would be observed at Service: the same standard of behaviour should be required, and Choristers should be taught that the Church rehearsal is an act of worship equally with the Service. A disorderly rehearsal is the best training ground for a disorderly Service.

Though it is best for the " spade-work " to be done in the practice room, still a certain number of rehearsals in Church are undoubtedly necessary.

The acoustical conditions and the organ accompaniment alone make this requisite, and also the rehearsal of behaviour is not without its value.

It cannot be denied that the office of a Choirboy is to some extent unnatural, and not without its dangers; it is difficult to prevent the necessary familiarity with sacred things from breeding the proverbial result, and it is only by the most strict insistence on the sacredness of the Church and all that belongs to it, that the danger can be avoided. No mere set of rules or system of punishments will be effectual: a far more powerful agency is the force of association. If a boy is taught to associate all his surroundings in Church with a symbolic meaning and a definitely religious purpose, he will unconsciously come to regard them with reverence. Boys are not naturally irreverent, only they are often thoughtless, and their attention is easily diverted. Long Services place a severe strain upon their self-control, so that they require every possible assistance, by serious appeal to the best that is in them.

It is the height of folly, if nothing worse, to sentimentalize over Choirboys, and regard them as budding angels: and it is equally unjust to regard them as so many imps of mischief who have to be coerced into some semblance of decency. Of course the ideal Chorister is merely a normal, healthy boy, and he should be treated as such.

The prominence of a Chorister's position in Church, however, renders any faults of behaviour very noticeable, and very offensive: such faults are therefore the more carefully to be repressed. But in many Churches it is only fair to say that the demeanour of the Choirboys is such as to put to shame that of the senior members, and of many of the Congregation, and sometimes—be it said with bated breath—even of the Clergy themselves. Where Choirboys are ill-behaved, the fault is more often than not to be found with those who are responsible for their training and for setting them a good example.

The dangers of conceit or priggishness are not so great as is often supposed, nor is there any serious danger of boys becoming bored with religion and sick of Church-going if they are wisely handled: all these things may easily be obviated by the exercise of judicious influence, and the greatest force will be the encouragement of a true *esprit de corps*—all for the Choir, nothing for self.

The time of a boy leaving the choir generally coincides with what is one of the most difficult and dangerous periods of his life; and it is a reproach to Clergy and Choirmasters alike, if boys are neglected at this period. If a boy is allowed to feel that as soon as his voice is broken the Church has no further need of him, is it to be wondered at that he gives up his Church-going ? Boys at this age are peculiarly shy and self-conscious, and the first few Sundays out of the choir are a severe trial to the best of them. This is the time when they specially need help and encouragement. The ice should be broken gradually, so as to make the break in continuity of Church life as slight as possible. One good plan is to find every boy some " job " he can take up directly he leaves the choir; this can be arranged in almost any Church; he can, for instance, act as a librarian and put out music, or can be used in many other ways. Anyhow, he should not be taken straight out of the Choir-stalls and put down in a pew and left alone. Various organizations for ex-Choristers may help to solve the difficulty, such as ex-Choristers' Clubs and Reunions; institutions like the Boy Scouts; special seats in Church reserved for Old Boys; corporate Communions on stated dates. All these things help: but the most successful plan for dealing with ex-Choristers is probably their employment as Servers at the Altar. In this capacity they retain a definite official connection with the Church, and are encouraged in the habit they should already have formed of regular Communion. The work itself nearly always seems to interest them, and they regard it as a privilege to be allowed to undertake it. Matters should be so arranged if it is possible, and the custom of the Church permits, that every suitable Chorister on leaving the Choir should immediately have the opportunity of becoming a Server. He should not have to wait for his turn; if he is to be kept firmly united to the Church, there should be no break at this time. To make room for new recruits, older boys should be asked to give way, it being assumed that they will by then have passed through the most critical time, and be ready to lend a helping hand to the juniors by standing aside in their favour.

Nevertheless all old boys should be kept touch with, and as far as possible be employed in definite Church work. One of the greatest difficulties which the Church has to face at the present time is its admitted failure to attract men: by means of the ex-Choristers alone it should be possible in any parish to form a strong, though perhaps small nucleus, of keen young Churchmen, who will by their attachment to the Church exercise a real influence on parish life. Ex-Choristers, too, undoubtedly form the very best source of supply for Choirmen, and from this point of view alone they are well worth looking after.

To summarize the conclusions arrived at, it will appear, then:

1. That Choirs are almost a necessity, but that they should be confined to boys (or women) singing in unison, unless there is sufficient material and equipment to enable a well-balanced four-part choir to be organized and maintained.

2. That nothing further than this should be attempted unless there is a reasonable prospect of surmounting the difficulties which are bound to be met with.

3. That anything in the nature of elaboration should only be attempted with a first-rate equipment, and in suitable surroundings.

4. That some system for dealing with ex-Choristers should form an integral part of the organization of every choir.

The heading of this chapter is " Quires and Places where They Sing," and in the latter category we may fairly include the body of the Church. Congregational singing is one of the favourite battle-cries of the day. There are those who would have us believe that here is the panacea of all evils, that if only it were not for our choirs all would be well. It is interesting to note how fashions change in ecclesiastical matters: time was when the surpliced choir was supposed to be the last word in improvement; but now it is getting into disfavour, and we find a tendency to revert to the use of women, and to re-establish the West Gallery Choir and Organ. It is simply a case of reaction against a tendency which had gone too far in the opposite direction; and people who advocate congregational singing to the exclusion of everything else are apt to talk a great deal of nonsense. Of course the congregation ought to sing, in the proper places: nothing is more inspiring than the good congregational singing of a well-known hymn, and plenty of music of this kind ought to find its place in every Service. But really good congregational singing of anything except hymns is almost unknown in this country. The reason is not far to seek: the average congregation is not sufficiently interested in the matter to take the necessary trouble to sing well. Yet if rehearsals are necessary for the selected musical members of the congregation, who are called the Choir, how can they fail to be necessary for the rank and file who have no special musical skill ? Well-known hymns most people can manage, and a certain amount of plain-song, such as Marbeck, may at times be found practicable: but with the Psalms, all that the congregation can be expected to do is to " join in " as best they can. Then congregational singing to be effective should be in unison. Now English people do not like singing in unison: edicts or exhortations are powerless to prevent the elderly lady from " singing seconds," or the lusty churchwarden from putting in his " bit of bass." Congregational practices may occasionally be satisfactory, but they more often fail after a few weeks, because people are not keen enough to attend them.

There are a certain number of people in every Church who demand what they call " a hearty congregational Service," forgetting that the attainment of this ideal will involve certain obligations on themselves: others there are who cannot bear that there should be any music in which they do not take an audible part. Their efforts may not even be capable of being described as singing; it is quite sufficient for them to " make a cheerful noise," and this they keep up, to the intense annoyance of their neighbours, through Psalms, Services, and Anthems alike. Others there are who rather fancy their powers as vocalists, and wish to take their part, but who for one reason or another will not qualify as members of the Choir.

It would at any rate be a wholesome discipline for these people that they should cultivate " the listening ear "; all people in Church are used to the idea of joining in many of the prayers without taking an audible part in them, and there is no reason why they should not equally enter into the spirit of the music without actually attempting to sing it. Certainly they should have their part in the praises as well as the prayers, but why not listen to the Anthem as reverently and silently as the Sermon ? It is a curious paradox that it is generally the musical people who are content to be silent, and the unmusical who demand to sing ! Congregational singing has its great uses, and nothing can take its place. But if it is to be of real value it must represent conscious effort, and not be merely spasmodic and selfish. Organized effort in the direction of congregational practice might do much, if only congregations could be induced to take the matter seriously; but it must be remembered that rehearsed effects will always be liable to be spoilt by those who have not been to rehearsal, and one cannot make attendance at rehearsals a condition of attendance at Service. So that it is better in practice to rely on the simplest things alone. New hymn-tunes, when introduced, should be repeated frequently at short intervals, until they are thoroughly well known. It is useless to expect congregational singing with unfamiliar music: this merely degenerates into a desultory muddle.

It is questionable whether the demand for purely congregational Services—that is Services in which everyone can join in every part of the singing—is as great as some of its advocates would have us suppose. English people as a rule like " joining in " a tune they know, but it by no means follows that this is a conscious act of worship; and it is quite possible to lay too much stress upon what may, after all, be of little value as a religious experience, and may be hardly more (to borrow the title of an old collection of Psalmody) than a " Divine Amusement."

CHAPTER V

THE PART OF THE CLERGY

THE part of the Clergy in the rendering of the Musical Service is too often overlooked. Through force of convention many men persist in, or think they are bound to attempt singing the Priest's part, with its inflections, and monotoning the Prayers. Now many men who are excellent Priests have not a musical ear, and they would not dream of attempting to sing a song at a parochial tea. None the less as soon as they get into Church they are confronted with the fatal " G," and contentedly produce sounds which in another place would merely provoke ridicule.

It is therefore necessary, as a first step, that it should be decided whether or not a Clergyman is sufficiently musical to enable him to sing the Service in an edifying manner. If he is not qualified, no amount of persuasion should tempt him to use any other than the speaking voice. Unfortunately no one is so poor a judge of his own voice as the possessor of it: and a man must be guided in the matter by the candid opinion of others. In at least one diocese there is in force an admirable system, under which the Bishop insists on all

Ordination candidates going through a course in reading or singing the Service, under the guidance of an expert. This instructor has the authority to tell each man whether or not he is competent to sing the Service: and the candidates in their course of instruction are trained accordingly. It would be an excellent thing if such a system could become universal. The subject has been to some extent dealt with in a previous chapter, so it need not be further enlarged on here, but it is one of the most urgent matters for reform, and one of the defects that can most easily be remedied.

On practical grounds a serious objection to the elaboration of the Priest's part and indeed to the perpetual use of music of any kind is, that it affords no relief. As a fine picture looks best when surrounded by a plain wall, so music produces a greater effect if relieved by absence of music, that is either by silence or non-musical sound. Such matters as these are simply questions of artistic expediency: there can be no doctrinal significance in a monotoned Absolution, an inflected Collect, or a harmonized Amen. Granted, however, that a Clergyman is sufficiently musical to be able to sing the Priest's part well, it is an undoubted gain to the smoothness and unity of the Service.

Exactly what the Priest's part should be is a matter which needs some elucidation, and it is a subject about which a good deal of confusion of thought exists. Marbeck's name is often quoted as the final authority, but comparatively few people have an accurate knowledge of exactly what his famous book contains. As every Clergyman ought to know something of this book, and as the original is exceedingly rare, while accurate reprints are hard to be met with, a somewhat detailed description of it may be useful.

John Marbeck (or Merbecke) was born about 1523, and became a Chorister of St. George's Chapel, Windsor, in 1531, and later became Organist. For his adherence to the principles of the Reformation he narrowly escaped suffering at the stake. He died in 1591. The work on which his fame rests is entitled " The Book of Common Praier Noted, 1550." From this it will be seen that the Book of Common Prayer dealt with is that known as the " First Prayer-Book of Edward VI.," which came into use in 1549.

The music, so far as can be ascertained, was chiefly derived and adapted from that of the Latin Service Books, which were already in use. Marbeck's main object seems to have been to adapt the ancient melodies of the Church to the English words, though in some cases, such as the Nicene Creed and Gloria in Excelsis, it is probable that he provided his own music, in the same style. Archbishop Cranmer, who had so much to do with the preparation of the First English Prayer-Book, laid great stress on the desirability of simplifying the old plain-song, on the principle of one note to a syllable; and he had already himself issued a "noted" edition of the Litany. So that Marbeck's great object seems to have been the simplification of the old melodies, while retaining their leading characteristics. Be this as it may, there is no question that his book is of the highest authority, both as a work of reference, and as contemporary evidence of the original musical treatment of our English Service.

A description of the contents of the book will indicate variations in order and arrangement from our present Prayer-Book, and special allusion to these will not be necessary, though they prevent its exact applicability to our present Use.

The book commences with Mattins, where "The Quere with the Priest" monotone the Lord's Prayer. (It is worthy of note that the rubrical directions throughout the book presuppose the existence of a Choir.) Then follow Versicles and Responses:

Priest. O Lorde, open Thou my lippes. (Monotone, a third below pitch of the Lord's Prayer.)

Aunswer. And my mouth shal shew forth Thy praise. (Monotone, the same note.)

Priest. O God, make spede to save me. (Inflected, the same melody as now in use.)

Aunswer. O Lorde, make haste to help me. Glory be to the Father . . . world without end, amen. Prayse ye the Lorde. (The whole of this Response, now broken up, is monotoned, except the words "Prayse ye the Lorde," which are inflected.)

The Venite follows, and the first verse is noted

to a form of the eighth tone, and then comes the rubric " And so forth wyth the rest of the Psalmes, as they be appoynted." This should at once set at rest any doubt that may be felt by opponents of plain-song as to the ancient authority for singing our English Psalms to Gregorian tones. The Te Deum is set to a simplified form of the Ambrosian melody. Two settings of the Benedictus are given, both to Gregorian tones. Then " The Quere with the Priest " monotone the Apostles' Creed, immediately followed by the Lord's Prayer: the last two clauses are set as a Versicle and Response, the Priest alone singing " And leade us not into temptacion," and the answer being " But deliver us from euil. Amen." These and the following Versicles and Responses, identical with our present use, are set in the method of inflection we still employ; the principle is that the voice drops a minor third to the last note if the last word has more than one syllable: but if the last word is a monosyllable a rise is made, after the drop, to the intermediate note. The three Collects, which are monotoned throughout, conclude the Service.

" Euensong " is treated in an exactly similar way to Mattins. Then follows " For the tyme of Lent in the place of Te Deum, Benedicite," noted to a Gregorian tone; then " Quicunque Vult," noted to the fourth tone, exactly like one of the Psalms.

The next section is entitled " At the Com-

munion," and commences with "The Introite."
The specimen given is the first verse of Psalm 1,
set to a form of the eighth tone (this is the Introit
appointed in the First Prayer-Book, for Advent
Sunday); then the rubric "And forth with ye
Introite as is appoynted for the day." Next
comes the "Threefold Kyrie" set to a simple
Church melody; then the Gloria in Excelsis, followed by the Creed, the settings of both being
most likely original work. Then come fifteen
Offertory sentences, set to simple plain-song
melodies. Then follows "The Preface." This commences with Versicles and Responses as follows:

Priest. The Lorde be with you.

Aunswer. And with thy spirit.

Priest. Lift up your hertes.

Aunswer. We lift them up unto the Lorde.

Priest. Let us geue thankes to our Lorde God.

Aunswer. It is mete and right so to do.

Priest. It is very mete, right, etc.

The whole of the above are noted in full, but
noted in monotone, as are also the Proper Prefaces
which are given *in extenso.* The Sanctus is set
to simple plain-song, and is immediately followed
by the "Benedictus qui venit," which forms part of
it. Monotone is now the rule till the end of the
Consecration. Then comes the Lord's Prayer, set
to a plain-song melody, the last two phrases being
again a Versicle and Response. Then comes—

Priest. The peace of ye Lord be alwaye with you.

Aunswer. And with thy spirit.

Then the Agnus Dei set to plain-song. The Service concludes with sixteen " Post Communions," set to plain-song melodies in the same style as the Offertory sentences, the Pax Vobiscum, one Prayer, and the Benediction.

The rest of the book consists of a plain-song setting of the sentences " At the buriall of the Dead," with variants for certain parts of the Service " At the Communion when there is a Buriall."

From a study of the above details two or three conclusions may be reached. In the first place the musical requirements of the Priest's part are exceedingly simple; indeed, simplicity is the keynote of the whole book. They do not include inflections of the Gospels, Collects, Comfortable Words, Proper Prefaces, or even of the Sursum Corda (though this last may well be sung to the inflections in common use throughout the Western Church). They certainly give no authority to any undue elaboration of the music, and that though they definitely presuppose the existence of a Choir.

The Clergyman, however, even if he is not musical, has an important part to fulfil in his relation to the Choir and the Church music generally. On him rests the ultimate responsibility for the whole of the Service, and it is for him to say what shall or shall not be sung; if he cannot himself decide on musical questions, he can acquaint himself with the views of those who are qualified to advise him. On him, too, rests the ultimate responsibility for the well-being of the Choir; he can at least interest himself in their work, even though he may be unable fully to appreciate it. No Choir works well unless it has the personal interest and backing of the Clergy.

His relationship to his Organist is also of the greatest importance. Given a man of suitable calibre, the Clergy should see that he is given a considerable amount of direct control, for no man who is worth his salt will put up with needless interference. The only possible way to avoid friction is for the Vicar to trust his Organist: if he feels that trust to be misplaced, the sooner they part the better for both. Some Clergy make the mistake of expecting their Organist to be little more than an instrument to carry out their own personal wishes. This is not the correct relationship: in most cases the Clergyman is, from a purely musical standpoint, the inferior of the Organist: and he should realize that in purely musical matters he should be to a large extent guided by the expert. At the same time the Organist should recognize that the department in which he is specially interested is not the only one that comes under the discretionary power of the Vicar; that different interests are bound to clash, and that it is his duty, as far as his artistic conscience will allow him, to carry out the wishes of his superior officer; and he should never for a moment forget that the ultimate responsibility for the ordering of every detail of the Service rests with the Incumbent. But the whole question of happy relations turns on the personal aspect: if the Organist is difficult and touchy, or if the Vicar is dictatorial and unsympathetic, there is bound to be friction: but if both realize the need for co-operation and mutual help, all is well. The Vicar rightly expects loyalty from his staff, and the staff have an equal right to expect loyalty from their chief.

Sometimes, however, the Vicar is not musical, and the Organist cannot be regarded as an expert. Where this is the case it is indeed difficult to suggest the right course of action; it would seem that the only help that can be looked for is that which comes from outside. It is in such cases that some diocesan scheme for the organization and assistance of Church music would be most helpful, and a suggestion as to this matter is dealt with in the last chapter.* But until such assistance is forthcoming, the only possibility is to rely on such help as may be offered, and to do the best that circumstances permit.

Finally, there rests upon the Clergy one very important duty, which they alone can initiate, and which is far too often left undone. This consists in the periodical reconsideration of the ordering of the Service, for the purpose of ascertaining what features of its rendering in the particular Church are of value, what are unedifying, and in what directions improvement can be made. We are all

* See pp. 105, 106.

apt to go on in the same way, year after year, and our musical organizations need from time to time a sort of " spring cleaning." Bad habits are easily formed: slackness creeps in in matters of detail; long established customs are found to be without value; new possibilities suggest themselves. To correct these things *each detail of the Service*, as rendered in the particular Church, should be considered dispassionately, and as far as may be from an outside standpoint.

The inquiry that should be made would be somewhat on these lines: Each part of the Service should be reviewed in order and submitted to the tests, " Is the present practice edifying ? Can it be improved?" Starting with the Responses, each one should be considered in detail: whether the particular setting used is the best; whether habits of false accentuation or careless pronunciation have crept in; whether the pace is right; whether the pitch is kept. The General Confession, the Lord's Prayer, and the Creed should be gone through sentence by sentence, in order to find out any of those mispronunciations which are so apt to become a habit from frequent repetition. Take alone a few common pitfalls, such as " Our Father, 'chart in heaven," " Lead us not in 'temptation," " kingdom, 'power and the glory," " device' and desires," " w' ought to have done," " miserable 'fenders "; these are only a few instances of the kind of thing that is frequently to be heard. Then with Psalms, consider whether the selection of chants is good, and whether certain settings might not be improved; whether they are not rendered too quickly—they generally are; whether the words are clear, particularly those in the recitation and those which come at the end of each half-verse. Of the Hymns we should ask: Is the pace chosen the best ? Is the selection good, having regard to a sufficient choice of popular hymns ? Are any hymns too often repeated, or are any too seldom heard ? And so on with every part of the Service down to the smallest details. It is only by regular attention to such matters that a high standard can be maintained: if they are allowed to take their chance, it is certain that errors will creep in almost unnoticed.

Remembering that all music is an ornament and addition to the Service, and not a necessity, we are within reason to ask, of every piece of music that is used: " Does it add to the beauty and devotion of the Service ?" If it does not, then one of two courses is necessary—it must either be improved or be abolished.

CHAPTER VI

CHOICE OF MUSIC

WERE it possible to draw up a simple formula by which the merits of any piece of music could be tested, the greatest obstacle in the way of reform would be removed. But in music, perhaps more than in any other branch of Art, it is impossible to lay down any laws which are of universal application. And indeed the discussion of the æsthetic principles underlying the art of composition involves technicalities which would be outside the scope of a book intended only for the general reader. There are, however, a few general principles which may serve as some guide in the matter even to those who have little or no expert knowledge. To make these clear they will be illustrated by reference to well-known hymn-tunes (the numbers refer to *Hymns Ancient and Modern*) but it must be understood that they apply equally to larger specimens of music.

In the case of simple music, and especially music to be sung in unison, the main requirement is a *good melody ;* so that in estimating the quality of music of this kind it is important to consider the melody alone, without too much reference

74

to the harmonies. A hymn-tune or chant which depends for its effect mainly on its harmonies is seldom good for unison singing or for congregational purposes. A few characteristics of good melody may be enumerated, and though it must be understood that none of them is of universal application, yet some of them will probably be found to belong to any really good tune.

(*a*) A melody should have certain definite points of interest: in other words, it should not meander aimlessly, but should be directed into definite channels. In a short melody there may be only one or two of these points on which the interest is focussed; in a longer one they will occur from time to time. On their position in relation to one another much of the effect depends. But a melody without these " landmarks " will generally be flat and dull. These points of interest may be formed in various ways. Sometimes by a judiciously placed high note—*e.g.*, " Dundee " (221), where the high note in the third strain is the making of the whole tune; or " St. Magnus " (301), where the leap of an octave at the beginning of the last line brings the tune to a brilliant ending, which in this case so happily coincides with the words to which it is set. On the other hand, if a tune such as " St. Bernard " (177) is examined, the first line, with its climax on the E flat is very good, but this same note is the point of climax also in the second and third lines, so that it becomes tiresome by repetition, and the point of the first bold phrase is weakened.

Sometimes the interest centres on a point of musical form, such as a neat balance of phrase, or repetition of a phrase in the same or a different pitch. Good instances of this may be found in " Tallis " (208), " Canterbury " (151), or " Redhead " (184). Where the effect is intentional it is often excellent; but where it is ill-managed it often produces an effect of monotony—e.g., " Stockton " (213), where the repetition of A sharp, B, at the end of the third line, is very feeble and dull.

Sometimes the interest is in the scheme of keys. Perhaps it is incorrect to speak of this in regard to a melody only; but, as a matter of fact, any tune suggests certain harmonies by its very progression, and these implied harmonies exercise a great effect on its character. " Hollingside " (198) is a good example; the main feature of interest is the D flat in the fifth line, involving an unexpected change of key; the tune is also a good example of a melody held together by repetition, lines one, three and seven being almost identical and also lines four and eight; and yet there is no feeling of monotony. Many other examples of this interest of key system might be quoted, but their explanation is necessarily somewhat technical, and it must suffice in further illustration to refer only to " Bristol " (53), " St. George " (180), and " Old 104th " (167), this latter being, from this point of view, one of the most interesting, as it is one of the finest of the old Psalm tunes.

Sometimes the interest is focussed on a special

rhythm—*e.g.*, " Kocher " (224), or " Innocents " (175)—or a special metre—*e.g.*, " St. Gabriel " (19), " Harewood " (239), " Alleluia perenne " (296), and many others. Of course, this question of rhythm and metre is largely governed by the words, but very often an unusual rhythm gives the whole point to a tune, and the art of the poet is of the greatest assistance to the musician.

(*b*) A tune should have a good melodic flow, and should be eminently singable. The progression of melody may be " conjunct," that is moving from one note to another above or below it, but next to it in the scale; or it may be " disjunct," that is moving by a skip, and to a note that is not next to it in scale order. Some melodies move almost entirely conjunctly, such as " Wareham " (63), or " Maidstone " (240); others are full of disjunct movement, such as " Church Triumphant " (35), or " St. David " (352). The best tunes generally have a judicious mingling of conjunct and disjunct movement, and on the arrangement of this much of the singableness of a tune depends. An example of a practically perfect tune is Clarke's " St. Magnus " (301).

It is to be observed that the repetition of the same note does *not* constitute melody. A repeated note may often produce a good effect, but this is largely a question of the accompanying harmony: and as a general principle it may be said that the frequent use of repeated notes is, from a melodic point of view, poor and dull. This is one of the

chief weaknesses of the tunes of Dykes and his
school; tunes like " St. Bees " (260), or " Melita "
(370) from a purely melodic point of view are
very poor and barren.   They may have other
virtues, but that is a different matter.

The same need for melodic interest applies to
the inner, and particularly to the bass parts, when
a tune is criticized from the harmonic standpoint.
Dull part-writing is a sure sign of weakness.
Compare, for instance, the interest of the parts in
a splendid tune like Wesley's " Harewood " (239)
or Smart's " Misericordia " (255) with the poverty-
stricken alto part of " Stephanos " (254) or " Cairn-
brook " (595), or with the bass of " St. Oswald "
(274).   It must, however, be admitted that the
melodic test is the true one for hymns, and that
very simple accompanying parts are often the best,
as concentrating the interest on the main tune.
The finest results are obtained where interesting
writing is attained by simple means.

Though it has only been possible to touch on
the fringe of this subject, enough has now been
said to point out the kind of directions in which
inquiries should be pursued by those who wish to
form a critical opinion on the merits at any rate
of simple music.   It will be seen that some discipline of thought is necessary, and that it is not
sufficient to be guided merely by an untutored
fancy.   Too often people will choose music simply
because " they like it," without giving any serious
thought as to whether their taste is well-founded.

In Church music particularly, there is a great danger that the judgment may be warped by association. Everyone, for instance, probably has a certain fondness for the hymns that he sang as a child; we all like music which has been associated with some stirring or interesting event in our own lives, or which is connected with some pleasant or deep memories, such as Christmas and Easter Hymns: other music we like because it calls to our minds certain words with which it is associated. Influences such as these cannot possibly be disregarded, even were such a thing desirable: at the same time they are wholly independent of the merit of the music in question, and should not be confused with it. A reasonable attitude is necessary, and to attempt to divorce a well-known hymn from a popular tune, merely because it is not of a musically high standard, is fatal. For instance, no one could be justly blamed for protesting at the hymn "Eternal Father" being sung to any tune but the well-known one of Dykes, but this is quite another matter from admitting that it is a good tune in itself. At the same time there are tunes in common use which no amount of popularity can justify, and at any rate the question of association does not furnish an excuse for the introduction of new music which is of poor quality.

The first step will have been gained if no new music is introduced unless it is really good, and this should speedily have the effect of driving out the taste for the bad that is already in use.

With regard to the introduction of new hymn-tunes and chants, which so often raises violent opposition; though it is obvious that this must be done with discretion, still it must be remembered that even tunes like Monk's " Abide with me," and Barnby's " For all the Saints " were new not so very many years ago !

But new tunes ought to be introduced from time to time, if only for the sake of keeping up the interest of Choir and Congregation. The great secret of success is to repeat tunes frequently when they are newly introduced: good tunes are often not liked at first because they are unfamiliar, but if they are repeated on consecutive Sundays or at short intervals, they will soon become popular; if, however, a tune is sung on one Sunday and not heard again for perhaps a year, it has the disadvantage of novelty each time it appears.

It is now necessary to consider the choice of music for all the different parts of the Service.

1. *The Responses.*—In a musical setting of these the plain-song as given in Marbeck ought certainly to form the basis, being, as has been pointed out, little more than the natural inflections of the voice translated into musical notation. In what are usually called the " Ferial Responses " the old plain-song, with slight variants, generally appears in the treble part, and virtually forms a har-monized melody. Tallis in his setting puts the plain-song in the tenor part (as was the common custom of his day) and adds surrounding har-

monies in the other voices.   Where these Responses
are used it would seem to be in accordance with
the composer's intention that the congregation
should sing the plain-song only, the ornamental
harmonies being left to the Choir; this at any rate
produces a fine effect.   Most Cathedrals have their
own " use " in the matter of Responses: the variations usually consist chiefly of different harmoniza-
tions of the plain-chant, but sometimes they are
specially composed.   As a general rule, in Parish
Churches at any rate, it is best that the Responses
should be set in a simple form in which all can
join.

Mention must be made of a practice which
unfortunately survives in some Churches and even
Cathedrals of employing harmonized and inflected
settings to some of the Prayers.   The so-called
" Ely Confession " is familiar to most people, and
similar settings for the Confession and Lord's
Prayer in the Communion Service are often to
be heard, in some cases tricked out with the
most unsuitable harmonies.   Settings such as
these cannot be too strongly condemned; at
these solemn moments quasi-dramatic harmonies
and ornamental treatment are utterly out of place.
Such passages are in most cases far better said
plainly, in the natural voice: but if they must be
sung, it is essential that this should be done quite
simply in monotone on a low note, so as to be as
little removed from speech as possible.

2. *The Psalms.*—In considering the music of the

Psalms we are brought face to face with the question of Anglican or Gregorian chants, and this opens up the whole question of plain-song. The subject may well be approached with a certain amount of hesitation, for there is no question connected with Church music which arouses so much controversy, or excites such warmth of feeling in the advocates of the rival methods. And it is just because they have been allowed to become rivals that the mischief has arisen; for, indeed, the truth is that there is room for both systems, and there is no reason why one should be exclusive of the other. Another difficulty is that, for reasons into which it is not necessary to enter, the use of plain-song has been allowed to become more or less a party badge, and is almost regarded as if it had some doctrinal significance. This is not the place for a lengthy discussion of the respective merits of the two systems;* but a certain amount of confusion is not infrequently met with as to what plain-song really is; so it may be well to point out that the term includes all Church music of a certain type, whether settings of Masses, Hymns or Psalms, and, broadly speaking, its characteristic features are:

1. That it is entirely unison music.
2. That it is not divided into bars of equal length.
3. That the length of notes is not fixed as in

* For a full but concise account of plain-song, see the pamphlet, " Plain-Chant and Faburden," by Godfrey Sceats, published by The Faith Press.

modern music, but that they may be increased or shortened according to the words to which they are sung.

4. (Arising from the above.) That the rhythm is free.

5. That the melodies all belong to early or medieval times.

The converse to plain-song is not specially Anglican music, but *all* music which is (1) in harmony; (2) divided into bars; (3) with notes of fixed length and accent; (4) of determined rhythm. Such music dates, generally, from a period not much before the middle of the sixteenth century.

The advocates of plain-song claim for that system:

1. The authority of tradition. Certain plain-song melodies were probably in use, in much the same form as we now have them, in conjunction with Christian Services of the earliest times, and some go back to an even earlier origin in the worship of the Temple. So that it is claimed that plain-song is the traditional musical language of the Catholic Church.

2. It is held that the Church ought to have music of a style quite distinct from anything else, and that this is best achieved by confining the choice to music of this special type, which is never associated with secular words; further that the suitability of the music in itself is so great as to make it superior to any other for this purpose.

3. As a setting for the non-metrical version of

the Psalms it is claimed that the system is the best, and indeed the only possible one, allowing as it does a variation in the length of each note, and the accentuation of each phrase according to the natural speech rhythm.

4. It is claimed that its simple character renders it more congregational than any other system.

The upholders of " barred music " on the other hand claim:

1. That the Anglican Church has a noble school of music of its own which it is its special duty to conserve, and that while ancient tradition has its great value, this should not prejudice subsequent developments.

2. That it is absurd to ignore all that has happened in the world of music since the sixteenth century, and to confine ourselves to the efforts of an age when music, in our modern sense, can hardly be said to have existed.

3. That the supposed advantage of plain-song as a setting for the Psalms is more apparent than real, and that as a matter of fact good Anglican chanting does not distort the words more than plain-song. That whatever inevitable drawback there is in the Anglican chant is more than compensated by the variety and intrinsic beauty of many of the specimens available; and that it can interpret the meaning of the Psalms, by the provision of suitable music, in a way that is impossible with the cold, colourless inflections of the plain-song melodies.

4. That plain-song is doubtless effective when used with Latin words, but that it does not suit the English tongue. In support of this they point to various inherent differences between the two languages, such as the Latin preference for " feminine endings " and words of more than one syllable, as against the monosyllabic character of the best English, and particularly that of the Prayer-Book Psalter.

5. That plain-song never has been and never will be generally appreciated by the English. This view is corroborated by the undoubted fact that as soon as the English language began to be used in our Service, so soon did the use of plain-song begin to fall out, even though an official attempt was made to graft it on to the English Liturgy. That in practice it is not found that congregations sing plain-chant any better than " barred music," and that as a matter of fact the " free rhythm " is a hindrance rather than a help to a congregation.

These are the main lines of argument, and there is much to be said on both sides; it is useless to attempt to give a verdict, for it is certain that neither system will oust the other. Much depends upon the standpoint of the person who has to make the decision, and general advice is quite useless. It is necessary, therefore, to regard the two systems side by side, not as antagonistic, but as parallel, and to consider briefly the applicability of each to the different parts of the Service.

But first one point must be emphasized. If

plain-song is to be used, let it be treated as plain-song should be, and let it not be " Anglicanized." It is utterly inartistic to graft on to plain-song a fixed rhythm, which is quite foreign to its nature, and destroys its most valuable and characteristic feature; and it is equally disastrous to clothe it with harmonies and accompaniments containing chords that are alien to its spirit. Fortunately the days of the old " Helmore's Psalter," sung in nearly as strict time as any Anglican chant, and accompanied with illustrative chromatic harmonies on fancy stops, are almost a thing of the past. But the danger is still with us; and if we want plain-song, the only consistent thing is to accept it in all its severity and purity: any attempt to make it sound " pretty " by tricking it out with fancy ornaments can only end in complete disaster.

To turn, then, to the actual rendering of the Psalter; where plain-song is adopted, our choice is confined to the so-called Gregorian tones, with their various endings. Though these are of a slightly different character, they cannot be distinguished from one another as possessing any peculiar emotional appeal; they are essentially " colourless " and not descriptive; and in this feature lies their special charm, and " atmosphere." When well rendered, plain-song chanting of the Psalms can be most beautiful; but anyone who adopts the system, thinking it will be easy, makes the greatest mistake. It requires the utmost care and intelligence if the rendering is to be tolerable, as by its very nature so much has to be left to the discretion of the individual. But given the specially trained Choir and the expert accompanist, it can satisfy the ear of the most critical musician.

The Anglican chant is essentially a compromise. There is no need to enter into the question of its origin: the thing itself is well known, and has become crystallized into a musical phrase of a definite number of bars and a more or less definite rhythm. To make it available for verses of different length, certain notes in each part of the chant are capable of indefinite prolongation as " reciting notes," and in this particular it is similar to the plain-song chant. But the rest of the chant is, in its essence, of determined rhythm, whereas the plain-song is free. Now it is obviously impossible to fit non-rhythmical words correctly to strictly rhythmical music: if an attempt is made to do this, we at once arrive at that hard, square type of chanting, characterized by what is contemptuously spoken of as the " Anglican thump." But such a treatment is *not necessary*, though it has unfortunately become more or less stereotyped. The rhythmic character of the chant should, in fact, be regarded rather as an outline, which is capable of infinite modification; naturally strong accents may be modified; notes, even in the " strict time " parts, may be shortened or lengthened; in fact, the whole chant should be regarded rather as a formula than as a fixed thing, the bar-lines, both in the Psalter and in the chant itself, being looked upon as marks of position, to guide the eye, rather than as connoting any fixed accent or duration. Any amount of liberty may then be allowed, provided that the musical feeling of the chant is not destroyed. If treated in this way there is no reason why the words should be distorted with Anglican chants any more than with Gregorian. The ordinary pointed Psalters are responsible for a good deal of the stiffness and lack of flexibility that is commonly associated with this system, and the time is ripe for a fuller recognition of the adaptability of the Anglican chant to a greater elasticity of treatment.

To sum up the matter, the truth is that either plain-song or Anglican chanting may be treated so that it distorts the words, and either may be treated so that the natural speech rhythms are preserved. Many of the faults that are to be found lie far less in the method chosen than in its manner of application.

As to the choice of Anglican chants not much need be said. It is only necessary to caution the unwary against setting an ordinary Choir to sing chants with high reciting notes, and to counsel the choice of chants of a simple and diatonic character; also to point out that no chant can be properly judged until it has been sung several times in succession: an effect which may be pleasant at a single hearing will speedily become wearisome if several times repeated.

3. *The Canticles.*—Where the Psalms are chanted, the Canticles should, if possible, be slightly differently treated; and the essence of such treatment is that it is more or less continuous, rather than one phrase repeated for each verse. Continuous treatment of the simplest kind is found in settings like Goss in A (Morning and Evening), or S. S. Wesley's setting of the evening Canticles (on almost plainsong lines), in F. Then there are arrangements of the Gregorian tones with certain verses in "Faux-Bourdon," which provide an excellent form of setting: and there are continuous plain-song settings like the Ambrosian Te Deum. A slightly more elaborate type of setting is provided by some of the older "Services" of the Cathedral type, such as those of Boyce and Arnold, or such settings as Rogers in D; and there are plenty of good modern settings which are quite as easy as these, such as Smart in G, or Somervell in F.* Services of this type may be introduced in any Parish Church where there is a complete Choir, and if frequently repeated could be learnt without difficulty by the congregation. When we come to more elaborate Services, in which the capacity of the congregation need not be considered, except as listeners, a large number of settings are available, of all degrees of difficulty and of merit. In selecting Services for Parish Churches, it is well as a rule to give the preference to those which do not indulge

* For a fuller list of simple "Services" see Appendix A.

in frequent repetitions of the words, or long organ interludes: it is also well to aim at simplicity rather than elaboration, which is a frequent cause of offence to the congregation.

4. *Communion Services.*—After the Reformation the practice of Choral Communion, except as far as the Creed, almost died out in England, except in a few places; consequently hardly any complete Communion Services of the " Cathedral type " were written. So that, with the general revival of Choral Celebrations during the last fifty years, it is necessary to rely for settings either on adaptations of plain-song to English words, on adaptations of foreign Masses to English words, or on modern settings.

As to plain-song, Marbeck's setting should find a place in every Church, not only on account of its intrinsic merits, which are considerable, but because it has a peculiar claim to be regarded as the official English setting of the Communion Service. It should hardly be necessary to add that it should invariably be sung in unison, or perhaps with occasional portions in Faux-Bourdon, and that harmonized settings, barred in strict time, are quite incorrect.

Turning to adaptations of foreign Masses, it is found that these are seldom successful. The difficulty of translation, when the English text has to be adhered to accurately, is almost insurmountable. Further, many of these Masses breathe an atmosphere which is hardly in accord with the traditions of the English Communion Service. However, such settings will not require much consideration, for they are commonly too long and too elaborate for use with an ordinary Choir. Some of the most successful are the adaptations of the Masses of Palestrina and his school: and these, where properly rendered, indeed abound with the true religious spirit which characterizes the best of the music we employ in our Services.

Modern Communion Services exist in abundance. Of simple settings a few really excellent examples have been written, such as Smart in G or Somervell in F; but there is great need for more of the same type. There are unfortunately also a number of Communion Services whose only merit, if it be a merit, is that they are easy. More elaborate Services abound, and there are many splendid specimens in the works of Stanford, Garrett, Selby, and others: perhaps for all round excellence it would be difficult to name a better setting than Smart in F. Such Services, when they can be rendered properly, should be the highest goal at which Choirs can aim. But there are many Services which rely on sensational effect or cheap sentiment rather than sound musicianship and which are nothing less than a desecration of the most sacred Service with which they are associated. As the Communion Service inspires some of the finest of our Church music, so it brings into existence some of the most flagrantly bad. Therefore there is no portion which demands the exercise of greater care in the matter of selection. As a general rule it is best to avoid settings which are quasi-dramatic, or which aim at startling effects, and to choose rather those which are dignified, reverent, and restrained. Above all things the least suspicion of vulgarity must be shunned like poison.

5. *Hymns.*—Hymn-tunes may be divided roughly into three classes:

(*a*) Plain-song tunes. In dealing with these, much that has already been said with regard to the Psalms will apply. Devotees of this kind of music will find much joy in the more florid specimens, which to other people will sound almost meaningless: but some of the simpler tunes, such as " Pange lingua," " Urbs beata," "Veni Creator," " Corde natus," or " Vexilla regis," have won their way into the hearts of most Church-goers, and seem the only suitable settings of the words. They should invariably be sung in unison, and with a free rhythm, and they require a tasteful accompaniment which can only be provided properly by one who has made a special study of their treatment.

(*b*) The " Psalm-tune " type is very numerous, and includes some of the very best specimens to be found in every collection. The earlier of these tunes are often severely plain, while later on we get a number of beautifully flowing melodies of a more florid description (particularly those belonging to the school of the eighteenth century). Most of these tunes are in a few simple metres, and are not specially written for any particular words, though in some cases, like " The Old Hundredth " or " St. Anne," they have become closely assotiated with them. The best of these tunes should form the backbone of all our Hymnody, and are the most generally satisfactory congregational music that we have. In early days it was often the custom to place the melody in the tenor part, and to surround it with harmonies in the other voices, instead of our present practice of placing the melody in the treble, and adding the harmonies below. This practice is akin to that known as " Faux-Bourdon," a similar treatment applied to plain-song.* Whether it was actually intended that the congregation should sing the tenor melody in octaves cannot be stated positively, but the effect of this method of rendering is very impressive; at the same time an opportunity is offered for interesting work to the Choir, without robbing the congregation of its part. It is a plan which presents considerable possibilities for future development, and a certain number of excellent modern examples have been written: several of the old Psalm tunes are given in this form in the *English Hymnal* and in the *Second Supplement to Hymns Ancient and Modern.*†

* For a full description of this, see Godfrey Sceat's pamphlet, " Plain-Chant and Faburden." The Faith Press.

† See also " The Tenor Tune Book " (Faith Press) and Athelstan Riley's Collection (Mowbray).

(*c*) Modern hymn-tunes, apart from the many excellent specimens which are written in the pure Psalm-tune style, may be distinguished as being generally written for special hymns, and as a rule they attempt to some extent to reflect the sentiment of the words in the music, so that the two become closely associated. For example, no one would think of using Dykes' tune for "Come unto Me, ye weary," to any other words, yet it would equally well, so far as metre goes, fit dozens of other hymns. It is obvious, however, that it is specially written for the one set of words, and with these it becomes wedded. So that the modern tune, in this sense, is not interchangeable as was the older type. This tendency to reflect the words as accurately as possible leads hymn-tunes of this style to become more like small Anthems, or as they have been called, "sacred part-songs." Special effects are sought by means of special chords, or by marks of expression, and a good deal of the interest is transferred from the melody to the harmonies. Such tunes as these have won an enormous share of popularity, which was greatly fostered by the issue of *Hymns Ancient and Modern*, with its many tunes of Dykes, Stainer, and their school. There is a tendency among the purists of to-day to condemn these tunes root and branch; and there can be no doubt that they have occupied far too large a place in our Hymnody. But the fact remains that several of them have become so endeared to congregations that it would be impossible, even were it desirable, to oust them; and though many of them are weak and sentimental, a considerable number are really good compositions, deserving of respect and admiration.

This is hardly the place to deal with the words, but, in extenuation of the much abused Victorian hymn-tune, it is only fair to say that many of the worst of them are admirably well-fitted to the verses to which they are set; and so long as these words, with their obvious insincerity of sentiment, are put into the mouths of ordinary congregations, it would hardly be possible to find a setting that suits them better !

Before leaving the subject of hymns a brief reference is needed to the attempt that has been made in some recent collections, and notably in the *English Hymnal,* to find in our traditional folk-song melodies a source from which popular hymn-tunes may be derived. There is no doubt that some of the experiments in this direction have been successful, and a certain number of fine tunes have been unearthed, which are well adapted to the purpose. At the same time it should not be forgotten that a tune is not necessarily beautiful or interesting because it is traditional, and that even some folk-songs are undeniably dull.

6. The Anthem, like the Service, provides some of the best, as well as some of the worst of our Church music. But here there is less excuse for a bad choice, for there is an enormous literature of good music available, of all degrees of difficulty,

ranging from the simple strains of Tye or Farrant, which can be sung by any Choir that can manage a hymn-tune, to the glories of Wesley which will tax the capabilities of the best. Much splendid foreign music, fitted to English words, is also available. So that there is no excuse whatever for a bad Anthem, more especially as this feature of the Service is an entirely unnecessary ornament. Special care, however, must be taken to avoid the trashy compositions which attempt to produce a grand effect by the most banal means. It is no drawback to a composition that it is simple and easy to perform: but when it is pretentious, and obviously written merely for the sake of cheap effect, it is nothing better than musical hypocrisy.

In general the choice of music has to be guided by environment: what may be suitable enough in one place is unsuitable or unworthy in another. Each piece of music introduced should be instinct with some definite purpose. It is, for instance, quite wrong to have an Anthem merely because it is the custom; again and again we must ask ourselves the question, " Is it edifying ?" And here, perhaps, is the best place for a word of warning against the practice which is so common in many Churches of filling up every possible moment with music. The Clergyman must even be " accompanied " while he walks to the Lectern; during the Communion we are treated to aimless improvisations, generally on the Voix Célestes, not to mention the irritating " few chords on the organ " that are put in at all sorts of places whenever opportunity offers. We need almost more than anything to realize the value of Silence in our Services, and in many Churches it would be an enormous gain if the so-called extemporizing of Organists were entirely abolished. Good extemporizing can, of course, be most effective and helpful, but the power is not given to everyone to excel in this direction, and nothing is more distressing than extemporizing which is not good.

The whole question of the choice of music is beset with difficulties. Those who cannot themselves form an independent judgment, based on adequate knowledge of the subject, will in the end have to rely on the opinion of the expert for their guidance. But where doctors differ, it is not easy to decide who is right; so that the only plan is to follow the advice of him who one feels is best qualified to give it. Were even so obvious a course as this consistently acted upon, the gain would be great; for the main reason why so much bad music finds its way into our Churches is not that the good is hard to discover, but that those responsible for its choice will not listen to any advice at all. The most fatal obstacle to reform is the man who says, " I am not musical myself, but I know what I like."

Admittedly Church music has other purposes than merely to gratify the ear of the cultured musician: but it is impossible to believe that the highest interests of religion can be served by bad

Art. Catchy tunes and feeble platitudes may perhaps attract the momentary attention of the flippant, or may even induce a pseudo-religious emotion; but good music has a higher ministry than this. When the best we can offer falls so far short of its great purpose, how can we be content to bring what we know perfectly well to be bad ?

CHAPTER VII

CHURCH MUSIC OF TO-DAY: POSSIBILITIES OF REFORM

CHURCH music in England to-day presents a somewhat complex problem. We have, on the one hand, a large and enthusiastic body of workers spreading over every part of the land, and accomplishing an immense amount of work: an increasing desire for good music in our Churches: a rising school of Church composers in the best style: a splendid tradition of native Art, kept alive on the whole with success in our ancient Cathedrals, College Chapels, and more important Parish Churches.

Side by side with all this, we see much waste of effort through lack of organization and technical equipment; a growing dissatisfaction amongst the more thoughtful members of the community with the existing state of things; the increasing production of much Church music that is utterly unworthy; and a certain hide-bound convention which keeps our leading centres of Church music from exercising their full influence.

The Oxford Movement, which did so much to improve the rendering of our Church Services, had at the same time certain effects which the light of subsequent experience has caused thoughtful people to regret. One of these developments was the institution of surpliced Choirs far and wide over the country, carrying with it a more or less conscious imitation of the Cathedral type of Service. It is unfair and unnecessary to disparage the surpliced Choir; indeed, experience has shown that the institution is of the greatest value if rightly used; but the order of procedure must be, " Form your Choir and teach them to sing, and then put them into surplices." Too often the process has been reversed, and the surplices have been relied on to produce the Choir.

So with enthusiasm: excellent and necessary as it is, it must not be relied on to produce results without instruction. It is too often taken for granted that because people " would like to join the Choir," they will be of value as members of it; and who does not know the enthusiastic Choirman who never misses a rehearsal or Service, but whose efforts are the ruin of the singing ? Again, there are many Organists and Choirmasters who take up their work from motives of enthusiasm, but without sufficient musical equipment to enable them to tackle what they have undertaken. Consequently we are met by the great difficulty that it is necessary either to accept things as they are, or to face the unpleasant alternative of damping the efforts of the enthusiast unless he is also competent.

In order that the standard of performance in

Church music may be improved, one of two courses is necessary. Either to provide better, that is more fully trained material, so that a sufficiency of good teachers, good players, and good singers may be forthcoming, or to prescribe for our Choirs and Organists a simpler diet, and restrict their efforts to such music as they can render adequately. The first course would be productive of a great raising of the standard of music throughout the land, and the ideal would be within reach that every Church Choir should become the true nucleus of good music in each Parish, under the guidance of a competent musician. But we have a long way to go before this goal can be attained, and in the present state of Church finances it would appear to be well-nigh impossible of realization—for even musicians must live ! We are faced, then, with the other alternative—to cut our coat according to our cloth. And the first great reform that is needed is the sweeping away from our Church Services of all music that cannot be rendered adequately by the material available—that is, not only by the Choir, but by all who take part in the music.

With regard to the quality of music so often sung, and the prevalent toleration of, and even preference for what is bad, Choir, Organists, Clergy, and Congregations are all to blame in this matter. It is hard, if not impossible, to define precisely what is bad and what is good in Art: but when the problem is solved of excluding the music which

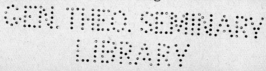

is *admitted* to be bad or poor, it will be time to deal with the classification of the remainder: Meanwhile, in every Church and Cathedral in the land, a certain amount of music is performed which no one can seriously defend except on the score of popularity. This means that the taste of the educated is constantly being sacrificed to please the ignorant. Those who know better keep on yielding to the weaker brethren, and so the vicious circle moves on. Vigorous action is needed by the authorities in weeding out what they know to be bad, whether it is popular or not.

The Cathedrals ought to be, and to a large extent are, models to show what can be done, under exceptional circumstances, to provide our Services with an ideal musical setting. On them primarily rests the duty of maintaining and handing down the traditions of the finest school of Church music in the world. But in addition to this they should form the central fountain of each Diocese, from which should spring the guiding force necessary to control, regulate, and advise the different Parish Choirs. By their daily Services they should set before the Diocese a constant object lesson as to how the best results can be achieved. By Diocesan Choral Festivals and similar organizations they should give practical demonstrations of what is needed, not by encouraging Choirs to attempt music they cannot manage, but by showing them how music that is within their reach can best be rendered. Cathedrals sometimes suffer from a certain torpor, and from that quiet and respectable dignity that is so dear to the hearts of Deans and Canons. The daily round of Mattins and Even-song is apt to have a deadening effect on all concerned, and unless a Cathedral Service is to degenerate into mere mediocrity, it is necessary that it should constantly be galvanized into new life by the introduction of fresh music and new ideas. The old traditions must, of course, be faithfully preserved, for they are our sacred and time-honoured heritage, but, in addition to this, modern thought and development must be welcomed, and the music be regarded as a living thing, and not a mere survival of the past. Above all, Cathedrals should never fail to set the highest standard in the matter of reverence, and of perfect rendering of the simple parts of the Service. The effect on a country Choir of a Cathedral Service which is deficient in such matters is simply disastrous, for it at once lowers the whole standard of their ideals.

The remedy for all these ailments is the same—Education.

Perhaps the most valuable educative force that can be found in matters of Art is criticism. Well-informed criticism is the basis of all true reform, but such criticism must be constructive: mere carping fault-finding, which can suggest no remedy, is worse than useless and is justly resented. But musicians are proverbially thin-skinned, and in the case of Church-music there is a too common tendency to resent criticism of any kind, however well-informed and well-deserved. Church music is held to be more or less sacrosanct, and it is too often regarded as not only unfair but almost irreverent to compare the music of the Church with that of the concert room. But there cannot be two standards of excellence, and such things as bad tone, out-of-tune singing, indistinct articulation, to say nothing of vulgar compositions, are certainly no more tolerable in a sacred than a secular building. Yet such evils are prevalent, and are often regarded as unavoidable: so much so that the cultured musician (who does not happen to be specially interested in matters ecclesiastical) scarcely regards Church music as a serious branch of the Art. The only chance of its taking its proper position in the musical life of the country is for it to emerge from the protecting shadow of religion, and to subject itself willingly to the same standard of criticism as is applied to other branches of the Art. Meanwhile, we have regretfully to admit that Sunday after Sunday all over the land compositions are performed of a character and in a manner that would not be tolerated on a concert platform. Is this right ? It means no less than that we are offering in the service of God music which we ourselves would not pay sixpence to listen to elsewhere !

So that the first step for all concerned in Church music is to humble themselves to listen to criticism, and to realize that what is not good enough for men cannot be good enough for God. When this spirit is attained they will have gone a long way on the road to progress.

The educative process will have to be applied to all concerned in the rendering of Church Services.

The Choir needs education chiefly on the technical side; they must learn to realize the great essentials such as correct voice-production, clearness of pronunciation, maintenance of pitch, balance and blend, and so forth; and they must be taught that without these things the rendering of any music, however simple or however elaborate, can never be even passable. Much, of course, depends upon the individual power of the Choirmaster, but far more might be done than has been. The value of movements like the Competitive Musical Festival is enormous, and it has been shown again and again that even remote villages can produce Choral societies to whose singing it is a joy to listen. But the movement has not yet greatly influenced Church Choirs, and there is need for its further extension in this direction. Much more use, too, might be made of Diocesan Associations of Church Choirs, which should aim more at education and less at grand united Services, where individual faults are apt to be covered up in a fine general effect. Further, we need something like a system of Diocesan Inspectors of Church music, or Diocesan Choirmasters, men of practical experience and ability, whose time should be devoted to going about the Diocese helping and criticizing and generally working for the betterment of Church music. This work should not be left to amateur effort, it is too serious; and considering the important place that is allotted to music in our Services, it surely should not be beyond the means of the Church to provide this most necessary equipment.

Choirs and Organists alike suffer from the tremendous drawback that they so seldom have the opportunity of hearing the efforts of other people. They all need far more object-lessons, for how can they be blamed for perpetuating what is bad, when they never have the opportunity of hearing what is good ? Our Cathedral Choirs might be better employed if, instead of always singing their daily Mattins and Evensong with, perhaps, a congregation of half a dozen old ladies, they could occasionally visit other Churches and give a rendering of the Service which would be an object-lesson to the whole neighbourhood.

Organists and Choirmasters need education also. Here we are met by the great difficulty that in the majority of Church appointments the salaries paid are so small that a man cannot be expected to undertake an expensive course of training to qualify himself to hold them. Indeed, in a very great many cases, the appointments have to be filled by any amateur or " semi-professional " who may be available. Still, even before these conditions can be improved something might be done. A system of visiting Choirmasters, as outlined above, should be productive of much good; Organists' Associations, which are springing into existence all over the country, are, if wisely guided, capable of much, by means of free interchange of ideas and even by practical experiment. Isolation is one of the greatest enemies to progress, and Organists should be enabled to hear Services other than their own; even an occasional interchange of organ-benches would not be without value. The Church Organist is far too apt to get into a groove, and anything that can be devised to get him out of it is of value. It is of the highest importance for his success in dealing with his Choir, as well as in his relations with the Clergy, that the Organist should be a man of all-round cultivation. Many musicians, unfortunately, have few interests outside their Art, and this tends to a narrowness of outlook which is greatly to be deplored. It should be the aim of all Organists to fit themselves to meet their Clergy on terms of social and intellectual equality, and were such relationship general, more than half the difficulties met with would disappear. A suggestion which seems to offer possibilities is that it might sometimes be feasible to combine the office of Organist with that of Lay-reader; at all events, any steps that could be taken to give the office of Organist some official recognition and some reasonable security of tenure, together with a living wage, would greatly improve his position.

The Clergy above all need education. They are the ultimate arbiters of what shall be or shall not be in Church music; yet very often from force of circumstances they are less equipped than many of their congregation to form a sound judgment on musical matters. Being unable themselves to arrive at an informed opinion, they are only too apt to be swayed by the ill-considered advice of others. In every congregation there will be some who prefer what is bad because they have not the intelligence to appreciate what is good. It is well-known that malcontents of this kind make more noise than those who are satisfied, and the Clergy are far too apt to give way to their demands simply for the sake of a quiet life. How often do we hear some terrible tune excused on the ground that it is " Lady So-and-So's favourite "; or that some dreadful anthem is allowed " because the choir like it," or " Mr. Smith wants to sing the solo " ? The Clergy should remember that while such methods may possibly attract some people to Church, they assuredly keep others away, and it is certainly not right that the wishes of the thoughtful should be sacrificed to please a few ignorant clamourers. It is not by lowering our standards that we can make progress, but by presenting and striving for the highest attainable ideal.

An objection may be made that remedies like those suggested are impracticable: the weight of opposition would be too great, and there is no sufficiently strong desire for improvement. But no great reform was ever accomplished without the facing of serious difficulties; and once public opinion can be roused to the inadequacy of the present methods, a solution can be found.

The present has proved to be a time when many of our long cherished ideas have had to go to the scrap-heap, and we must realize that things that have been good enough in the past will not do for the future. The Church has to admit the need of reform from within, and it is absolutely necessary that Church musicians should face that part of the problem which specially concerns them. But before any reform can be accomplished, Congregations and Clergy must be roused from the apathy to which they have so long been subject. They must learn to expect and demand good music in Churches (and once more let it emphatically be stated that good music must not be confused with elaborate music). They must take Church music seriously, and not as a mere concession to custom, or a thing to be tolerated. Taste in musical matters has advanced by leaps and bounds in this country during the last few years. This improvement is as marked in the cottage as in the hall. Choral Societies, Local Orchestras, Elementary School music, Competition Festivals, even Pianolas and Gramophones have done an enormous work in making known to the general public the greatest works of Art. So that there is no longer any lack of appreciation of the best. But so long as we accept one standard for the concert room and another for the Church, so long will the evil go on.

Church music to-day contains so many hopeful

elements, and there is so much promise of good things to come, as well as a considerable amount of excellent attainment, that there is not the slightest reason for despondency. All that is needed is a firm tackling of the difficulties that remain.

Our Church music has been enormously affected by the war; Choirs have been depleted; other more pressing needs have diverted much of our attention from the subject; but it is only by giving the matter most earnest consideration that we shall be enabled to face and profit by the time of reconstruction that is to come. When it does come it will be the finest opportunity there has ever been for making a fresh start. Much of our past tradition, the bad as well as the good, has been scrapped, and it is for the Churchman of to-day to see that when the fabric is rebuilt, we utilize only the material which is of value, otherwise we shall merely be trying to recreate a dead thing. We must not only gather together our dry bones, but we must also breathe upon them that they may live.

APPENDIX A

CHOICE OF MUSIC

ANY attempt to compile a list of music suitable for choirs is beset with great difficulties. In the first place, it is almost impossible for any one person to become acquainted with all the material available; and, secondly, the suitability of any music entirely depends upon the conditions obtaining at the particular Church in question.

In the matter of Anthems it is felt that there would be little value in any recommendations: the field of choice is so wide that any comprehensive list would defeat its own object by being too large; while a small selection would be of little use, and would possibly do more harm than good, owing to the necessity of omitting mention of much which might well find a place in a choir's repertory.

But with Services the case is somewhat different, and it is thought that a list of some of the simpler Services would be useful; for it is often not easy to find suitable Services for ordinary choirs, which are musicianly and reverent, and at the same time not too difficult. Of the more elaborate Services there is no need to speak, for Choirmasters of the more advanced choirs should be fully capable of making their own selection. But an attempt is made to classify a few settings under two headings: (*a*) The very simplest Services;

(*b*) those which are not beyond the capacity of any ordinary choir, where the parts are complete and there is a proper Organ.

The lists do not profess to be at all complete or comprehensive; but the music included in·them is all " safe " and suitable.

Those who desire further guidance in the matter of choice of music are referred to the *Lists of Services and Anthems* issued by the " Church Music Society " (Humphrey Milford), which can be obtained at a small cost.

A.—The Simplest Services

GOSS in A. Morning and Evening. *Novello.*
> Mostly in the form of a Chant Service, of the simplest possible character. There are two versions of this Service, in Harmony (P.C.B.,* 274, 275, 254, 327), and in Unison (P.C.B., 267, 244, 245, 342).

GOSS in D. Nicene Creed only. *Novello.*
> Very simple Unison Chant Service; hardly more than a few inflections; can easily be sung by a Congregation alone.

HAYNE in G. Communion (without " Benedictus " and " Agnus "). *Novello.*
> Very simple plain four-part Service, suitable for small choirs, and presenting no difficulty whatever.

HELMORE. " Te Deum." *Weekes.*
> Four settings (Nos. 1, 2, 3, 4) to short chants.
>> These are nothing but exceedingly simple chants, which are specially written to avoid the difficulties incidental to pointing the " Te Deum " to ordinary chants.

NICHOLSON in G. Communion (complete). *Faith Press.*
> Written with a view to the needs of small or incomplete choirs. Mostly in Harmony, but could be sung in Unison.

OUSELEY in C. Communion (without " Benedictus " and " Agnus ") (P.C.B., 221). *Novello.*
> A short simple four-part setting, not beyond the powers of a small choir.

---

* *Parish Choir Book* Series.

PEARCE IN D COMMUNION (complete). *Hammond.*
Creed in Unison; the rest in simple four-part harmony of moderate compass, and presenting no difficulty.

MARTIN SHAW (MODAL SETTING). COMMUNION (complete). *Curwen.*
A very simple Chant Service; there is no difficulty beyond the somewhat unusual tonality.

SMART IN G. MORNING, COMMUNION, AND EVENING (without " Benedictus " and " Agnus "). *Metzler.*
A very good Service of the simplest type; most suitable for ordinary choirs; it presents no difficulty, but at the same time is most effective.

S. S. WESLEY IN F. MORNING AND EVENING (" Chant Service Letter B."). *Novello.*
This beautiful Service is perfectly simple and congregational, and is partially built on plain-song lines.

It is suggested that in the case of Communion Services which do not include settings of the " Benedictus " and " Agnus Dei," Merbecke's setting should be used.

B.—SERVICES SUITABLE FOR AN ORDINARY CHOIR

The following Services are all easy, straight-forward and short, and none of them are beyond the powers of an average Parish Church choir, in which all the parts are adequately represented:

ARMES IN B FLAT. COMMUNION (complete). *Novello.*
A Unison Service with plenty of variety, and an interesting. independent Organ accompaniment.

ARNOLD IN A. EVENING. *Novello.*
An old-fashioned Cathedral Service; quite suitable for Parish Choirs, and attractive to the Congregation.

BOYCE IN A. MORNING. *Novello.*

BOYCE IN C. MORNING. *Novello.*
Both Services are good and attractive specimens of the Classical Cathedral style, but are quite easy and suitable for Parish Choirs.

BREWER in E Flat. Morning, Communion (complete), and Evening (P.C.B., 588, 602, 661). *Novello.*

This Service presents no serious difficulties, and though it is of a more ambitious character than many of those named, it will repay the trouble that is spent in mastering it. Suitable for Festival occasions, it is highly effective in proportion to its difficulty.

ELVEY in E. Communion (complete). *Novello.*

A plain Church-like Service on simple lines.

GARRETT in F. Morning, Communion, and Evening (" Service No. 3 "). *Novello.*

A simple musicianly Service, with a good deal of Unison, and well adapted for general use.

HARWOOD in D. Communion (complete). *Weekes.*

A very beautiful Service which, though not extremely easy, yet contains no real difficulties, and amply repays any trouble spent in learning it.

KEMPTON in B Flat. Morning and Evening. *Novello.*

A very straightforward Cathedral Service, presenting no difficulty and suitable for ordinary use.

LLOYD in A. Evening. *Novello.*

A bright and attractive Service of Festival type, requiring a good Organ; written with a view to the needs of Parish Choirs.

LLOYD in E Flat. Morning, Communion (complete), and Evening. *Novello.*

A plain, reverent setting. The Morning and Evening Services are slightly more difficult than the Communion.

LLOYD in F. Communion (complete). *Stainer and Bell.*

Presents no serious difficulty, and is well-written and effective.

MACPHERSON in D. Evening. *Novello.*

A bright Festival Service, not difficult, and very effective. Needs a fairly large choir and good Organ.

MACPHERSON in F. Evening. *Novello.*

Of interest to choirs and modern in feeling, but laid out on quite simple lines.

PARRY in D. Morning, Communion, and Evening (without " Benedictus " and " Agnus "). *Novello.*

A simple Service, largely in Unison with independent Organ accompaniment. It contains much effective writing.

ROGERS IN D. MORNING, COMMUNION, AND EVENING. *Novello.*

A quiet Cathedral Service presenting no difficulty. The Communion Service has been completed (except for the " Benedictus " and " Agnus ") by Sir F. A. Gore Ouseley, and is thus rendered available for ordinary use; but it is suggested that it will be found preferable for the Communion Service to be sung " Full " throughout.

RUSSELL IN A. EVENING. *Novello.*

A Service very much of the same type as Arnold in A; equally easy and effective.

SELBY IN E FLAT. COMMUNION (complete). *Novello.*

This Service is issued in two forms:
> For S.A.T.B. (four parts) (P.C.B., 484).
> For Boys' Voices (mostly Unison) (P.C.B., 483).

The setting is suitable for an average choir; it is eminently Church-like, and at the same time modern in feeling.

SMART IN F. MORNING, COMMUNION, AND EVENING (without " Benedictus " and " Agnus "). *Novello.*

The " Te Deum " is very easy, but the rest of the Service is on a much larger scale. The Communion Service is one of the finest there is, but it should not be attempted by any but a good choir.

SOMERVELL IN F. MORNING, COMMUNION, AND EVENING (without " Benedictus " and " Agnus "). *Novello.*

One of the best Services throughout for ordinary choirs. It is absolutely easy, very reverent in character, and at the same time attractive.

SOMERVELL IN D. EVENING. *Curwen.*

An easy Service of a more festal character than the above.

WALMISLEY IN D MINOR. EVENING. *Novello.*

One of the finest of all Evening Services; it is not exactly easy, but it is not beyond the capacity of an ordinary choir, and is an almost ideal setting.

LEE WILLIAMS IN C. COMMUNION (without " Benedictus " and " Agnus "). *Novello.*

Quite easy; good straightforward music, well adapted to an average choir.

S. S. WESLEY IN F. MORNING, COMMUNION, AND EVENING (" Cathedral Service "). *Novello.*

In the best pure ecclesiastical style, and without any difficulty. The Communion Service is incomplete, providing no setting of the " Gloria in Excelsis."

C.—Plain-song Music

MERBECKE.

　I. Edited by Basil Harwood. *Novello.*

　　(*a*) With accompaniment, melody printed in four-line notation.

　　(*b*) Voice part printed separately. (P.C.B., 784.)

　II. Edited by Royle Shore. (" Diocesan Music Series," No. 1.) *Novello.*

　　(*a*) Voice parts printed separately, small edition, modern notation.

　　(*b*) Accompaniment to the above, with notes on the " Art of Plain-Chant Accompaniment."

　　(*c*) Alternative accompaniment to the above, with optional Faux Bourdon and other vocal accompanying harmonies for the Choir. (With Scottish Supplement.)

　III. Edited by C. V. Stanford. *Novello.*

　　Voice part in modern notation, with accompaniment.

　IV. Voice part only, four-line notation. *Mowbray.*

　　Any of the above editions may be used; each of them vary slightly.

MISSA DE ANGELIS.

　I. Edited by Basil Harwood. (P.C.B., 784.) *Novello.*

　II. Edited by W. S. Vale. *Winthrop Rogers.*

Both editions are in modern notation, with accompaniment. A late plain-song setting, very attractive and tuneful, and extremely popular on the Continent.

MISSA REGIA. Edited by F. Burgess. (P.C.B., 861.) *Novello.*

Ascribed to H. Dumont (1610 to 1684), and adapted from the version in the *Solesmes Gradual.* Mainly syllabic in character; printed in modern notation.

MISSA SIMPLEX.

　I. Edited by F. Burgess. (P.C.B., 900.) *Novello.*

　　Printed in modern notation, with accompaniment.

　II. Edited by the Rev. J. W. Doran. *Mowbray.*

　　(*a*) Voice part only, printed in four-line notation.

　　(*b*) Accompaniment to the above.

This setting is taken from an old Choir Book supposed to have come from St. George's, Windsor, and some three years older than Merbecke's setting. It is the first known transcription of the traditional plain-song to the English Communion Service.

COMMUNION SERVICE: PLAIN-CHANT FROM THE SARUM GRADUAL. EDITED BY ROYLE SHORE AND E.G.P. WYATT. (" Diocesan Music Series," No. 3.) *Novello.*

> (a) Voice parts printed separately (modern notation) in small edition.
> (b) Accompaniment to the above.

This setting is somewhat more elaborate than Merbecke, but is mainly syllabic in character.

MAGNIFICAT AND NUNC DIMITTIS, SET TO GREGORIAN TONES, WITH VERSES IN FAUX-BOURDON OR EARLY ENGLISH HARMONIZED CHANTS. EDITED BY FRANCIS BURGESS AND ROYLE SHORE. (" Diocesan Music Series," No. 2.* *Novello.*

These settings provide a good method of dealing with the Evening Canticles, being interesting to the Choir and yet retaining a distinct part for the Congregation. They are of varying degrees of difficulty, but for due effect all of them need a good choir.

The " People's Part " of all the eight settings is published together in one small booklet. The complete settings are published each one separately in Novello's " Parish Choir Book Series."

---

* The " Diocesan Music Series " is being continued, and some other numbers have already appeared which will be useful to Churches desiring settings in which the Congregation can take part.

APPENDIX B

CHRONOLOGICAL CHART OF ENGLISH CHURCH COMPOSERS

Principal Composers of English Church Music.	*Contemporary English Sovereigns.*	*Contemporary Foreign Musicians.*
I. EARLY ENGLISH SCHOOL. Christopher Tye, c. 1508–1572 Richard Farrant, 1530–1580 Thomas Tallis, 1520–1585 John Merbecke, 1523–1585 ?	Henry VII., 1485–1509 Henry VIII., 1509–1547 Edward VI., 1547–1553 Mary, 1553–1558 Elizabeth, 1558–1603	Palestrina, 1515–1594 Monteverde (*founder of Opera*), 1566–1650
William Byrde, c. 1583–1623 Orlando Gibbons, 1583–1625	James I., 1603–1625	Carissimi (*founder of Oratorio*), 1580–1673
II. SCHOOL OF XVIITH CENTURY. Pelham Humfrey, 1647–1674 Michael Wise, 1648 ?–1687 Henry Purcell, 1658–1695 John Blow, 1648–1708 Henry Aldrich, 1647–1710 William Croft, 1678–1727	Charles I., 1625–1649 Commonwealth Charles II., 1660–1685 James II., 1685–1689 William and Mary, 1689–1702 Anne, 1702–1714	

III. SCHOOL OF XVIIITH CENTURY.		
John Weldon, 1676–1736	George I, 1714–1727	J. S. Bach, 1685–1750. *St. Matthew Passion,* 1729
Charles King, 1687–1748	George II, 1727–1760	
Maurice Greene, 1695–1755		Handel, 1685–1759. *Messiah,* 1742
John Travers, 1700–1758		
James Kent, 1700–1776	George III, 1760–1820	
William Hayes, 1707–1777		Mozart, 1756–1791
William Boyce, 1710–1779		Haydn, 1732–1809
James Nares, 1715–1783		
Jonathan Battishill, 1738–1801		
Samuel Arnold, 1740–1802		
IV. MODERN SCHOOL.		
Thomas Attwood, 1765–1838	George IV., 1820–1830	Beethoven, 1770–1827
Samuel Wesley, 1766–1837	William IV., 1830–1837	Schubert, 1797–1828
William Crotch, 1775–1847	Victoria, 1837–1901	Mendelssohn, 1809–1847. *Elijah,* 1846
Thomas Attwood Walmisley, 1814–1856		
Samuel Sebastian Wesley, 1810–1876		Schumann, 1810–1856
Henry Smart, 1813–1879		Spohr, 1784–1859
John Goss, 1800–1880		Wagner, 1813–1883
F. A. Gore Ouseley, 1825–1889		
George Garrett, 1834–1896		Gounod, 1818–1893
Edward Hopkins, 1818–1901		
John Stainer, 1840–1901		Brahms, 1833–1897

INDEX

BILLING AND SONS, LTD., PRINTERS, GUILDFORD, ENGLAND

Recent Publications at the Faith Press.

A SIMPLE COMMUNION SERVICE IN G. By SYDNEY
NICHOLSON, M.A., Organist and Master of the Choristers at
Westminster Abbey. Second Impression. Price 8d.

The only service published which combines really good four-part harmony
with simplicity.

MISSA DE ANGELIS in modern notation. Voice Parts, 3d.
Organ Copy, 1s. 6d.

The most widely used service in the west of Europe.

THE TENOR TUNE BOOK, a collection of descants, ancient
and modern, to well-known hymn tunes (other than plain chant)
in which special care has been given to include only melodious
faux-bourdons suitable for modern use. Quarter cloth boards.
Price 1s. 6d.

PLAIN-CHANT AND FABURDEN. By GODFREY SCEATS.
A most interesting and readable introduction to the subject, with
musical illustrations. Paper 6d.

A SELECTION OF COMMUNIONS adapted from the
Sarum Gradual by E. W. GOLDSMITH. Quarter cloth boards.
Price 8d.

Motet for All Saints, as used at Southwark Cathedral. **2d.**

Requiem Aeternam. The Communion Music in modern notation.
2d.

Ave Verum. By Mr. WILLIAM BYRD. 2d.

Te Deum, 8th Tone with faux-bourdon by VIADANA. 2d.

Te Deum to Ambrosian chants. E. W. GOLDSMITH. 2d.

Sanctus and Benedictus. By K. HENRY VI. and Mr. SHEPHERD.
4d.

De Profundis, for use at Requiems. 1d.

St. George for England, hymn for boys. 1d., Organ 3d.

PRINTED AND PUBLISHED AT

THE FAITH PRESS

THE FAITH HOUSE, 22 BUCKINGHAM ST., CHARING CROSS, W.C.2
MANCHESTER: 5 AND 7, GREENGATE, SALFORD.

Recent Publications at the Faith Press.

RELIGIOUS COMMUNITIES OF THE CHURCH OF ENGLAND. By the Rev. A. T. CAMERON, M.A. With Preface by the Duke of Argyll. The only history of the revival of the religious life in England. Fully illustrated. Price 7s. 6d. net.

"No such complete handbook has ever yet been compiled."—*Church Times.*
"A book of absorbing interest."—*Scottish Chronicle.*
"A valuable footnote to English ecclesiastical history."—*Contemporary Review.*
"It will be a surprise to most people to read of the extent of the operations. . . . There is no doubt that the Bishops of the Church of England have shown great weakness."—*English Churchman.*

THE MYSTERY OF THE KINGDOM. An Historical and Critical Exposition of the Revelation of S. John the Divine. By the Rev. C. E. DOUGLAS, S.F. With 160 illustrations of ancient symbolism. Price 7s. 6d. net.

"An able investigation."—*The Times.*
"Cannot fail to throw a great deal of light on much that is obscure."—*Church Times.*
"Much of the material employed is new, especially in connection with the prophetic mysticism of the Hebrews, and is handled deftly and firmly throughout."—*Saturday Review.*

LINKS IN THE CHAIN OF RUSSIAN CHURCH HISTORY. By the Rev. Dr. FRERE, C.R. An account of the ancient patriarchate suspended by Tsar Peter and revived in 1917. Price 6s. net.

"A tonic against despair."—*Church Times.*
"Sure of the welcome which it undoubtedly deserves."—*Expository Times.*

PRIESTHOOD IN LITURGY AND LIFE. By the Rev. A. H. BAVERSTOCK, M.A. Price 3s. 6d. net.

"No priest will read it without profit, and it may be for many of them an introduction to ascetic theology, enlightening them on many subjects on which they were not only ignorant, but of the existence of which they were hardly aware. . . . It may be said, without exaggeration, that this book is thoroughly good all the way through."—*Church Times.*

THE LITURGY OF THE EASTERN ORTHODOX CHURCH. Translated with Notes by the Rev. H. HAMILTON MAUGHAN, M.A. With 11 full-page illustrations. Price 2s. 6d. net.

"The student and the advanced scholar will alike profit from this excellent work."—*Asiatic Review.*
"The very book for the reader who may desire to assist at the Liturgy in any of the Greek Churches in England. . . . Eleven full-page illustrations are of special interest, taken as they are from sources that usually are not accessible."—*Church Times.*

PRINTED AND PUBLISHED AT

THE FAITH PRESS

THE FAITH HOUSE, 22 BUCKINGHAM ST., CHARING CROSS, W.C. 2
MANCHESTER: 5 AND 7, GREENGATE, SALFORD.